emotional currency

emotional currency

A WOMAN'S GUIDE TO BUILDING A HEALTHY RELATIONSHIP WITH MONEY

Kate Levinson, PhD

CELESTIAL ARTS
Berkeley

Celestial Arts and the Celestial Arts colophon are
registered trademarks of Random House, Inc.

Library of Congress Cataloging-in-Publication Data
Levinson, Kate.
Emotional currency : a woman's guide to building a healthy relationship
with money / Kate Levinson.
p. cm.
1. Women—Finance, Personal—Psychological aspects. 2. Money—
Psychological aspects. 3. Finance, Personal—Psychological aspects.
4. Women—Finance, Personal. I. Title.

HG179.L472 2010
332.0240082—dc22

2010020566

ISBN: 978-1-58761-068-4 (alk. paper)

Printed in the United States

Cover design by Betsy Stromberg and Toni Tajima
Interior design by Toni Tajima

This book is dedicated to my mother, Bobette Eckstein Levinson,

and my mother-in-law, Mildred Maloof Costa—

two women whose lives were so different, financially and otherwise,

but who shared the same openhearted generosity.

ACKNOWLEDGMENTS

I owe a large debt of gratitude to the many people who have taught me about money: my family, my friends, my clients, the women I interviewed for the book, and the women who have attended the Emotional Currency Workshops.

My thanks to Philip Fradkin for his introduction to Carl Brandt, who read my proposal and suggested it to Gail Hochman, his partner at Brandt & Hochman Literary Agents. Gail guided me so wisely through several edits and, in a moment of intense doubt, reassured me by telling me one of her money stories. More than any other words could have, her story showed me that there was value in the idea of this book. Gratitude to Marci Adamski for making the introduction to Julie Bennett, the acquisitions editor at Ten Speed Press, and to Julie who "got" the book. And my thanks to Veronica Randall, senior editor at Ten Speed, for carrying us steadily, the book and me, through the home stretch. Special thanks to Nancy Park for coming up with the name Emotional Currency for my workshops, which became the title of this book.

Many friends and professional editors, over lots of years, have made their marks on the chaos of words and ideas that has now become *Emotional Currency*. I thank them all, especially Francine Allen, Wendy Earl, Kathryn Frank, Catherine Lucas, Doris Ober, Rachel Remen, Jane Reynolds, Linda Spangler, and Margaret Wrinkle. I am especially indebted to Nancy Addess and Jean Blomquist, editors on the last drafts of the book, who continually asked for clarification, rewording, and reorganization. I truly couldn't have made it without all of you!

And to my beloved husband, Steve Costa, my gratitude for all that he has brought into my life. It was a very good thing that I'd discovered that money was emotional currency before he had the idea of buying

Point Reyes Books. Without having done some of my inner money work, I would certainly have said, "We can't! We don't have the money." And our lives would have been poorer. Instead, our world has been immeasurably expanded and enriched, but of even more value to me has been the deepening of our partnership.

I now have the privilege of being both an author and a bookseller. I thank the independent booksellers for continuing, against all odds, to be a vital part of bookselling in America. I know that this book would never have been published without their existence.

CONTENTS

Being clueless about money is no longer affordable.

INTRODUCTION:
Getting Started

F OR MOST OF MY LIFE, I thought money was just the tangible thing that we dealt with every day: cash, coin, check, and credit card. I wasn't supposed to have feelings about it, and when I did, I quickly pushed them aside. I took pride that I didn't let money dominate my life—as it did my father's—and I thought that my only dilemmas with money had to do with my not having enough of it and not being good with numbers.

Occasionally, I would try to educate myself about finances and pay attention to my money. I failed at each new approach to bill paying, record keeping, budgeting, investing, and saving. I spent years listening to the wrong people for financial advice and making poor financial decisions. All of these experiences reinforced my idea that I didn't "do" money, meaning I was only good at making it disappear, either by spending it or making bad investment decisions. I was a woman, after all, and for generations women have been told that they are not capable of managing money well. I was only too glad to buy into this stereotype.

We live in a culture that until very recently thought women's financial place was to be dependent on men. It taught, and often legally required, women to rely on their fathers, husbands, brothers, sons, and financial experts to handle their financial concerns. But for the past several decades, women in the United States have been entering new territory as we make, spend, save, invest, and manage money. Our financial management skills have not kept pace. It is abundantly clear, however, that relying solely on others to handle our money matters is not healthy; we need to develop our own skills and strengths in regard to money just as we have for decades in the workplace.

But "doing" money well goes beyond our need to learn traditional principles of money management and financial planning. We also need to understand and value the way we relate to money as women, and that includes our emotional relationship to it. Money in and of itself is not emotional. It's just a piece of paper after all, but it's a piece of paper that can hold powerful psychological and emotional meaning. For most women, money is laden with feeling. Some emotions, especially when we don't attend to them, can present obstacles in our dealing with money, and some can make money a vital and useful entity in our lives.

BECOMING CONSCIOUS ABOUT MONEY

What seems unbelievable to me now is that, even though I was a practicing therapist and knew well about the power of working with emotions, the concept of thinking emotionally about money had never occurred to me. I assumed my discomfort with money was caused by the amount I had and how I mismanaged it, never glimpsing that most of my money dilemmas had to do with my feelings and what it meant to me, as I had always had enough to cover basic expenses.

In order for us as women to come to our own wisdom and our own solutions about money, I believe it is essential for us to become conscious of our psychological and emotional relationships to it. For us to engage with money in ways that honor ourselves, the people and things we believe in, and the world—rather than just honoring money—we need to work with our emotional responses to it.

The dilemmas and choices women face in relation to money are multilayered, involving the inner states and needs of ourselves and others as well as the outer concerns and demands of ourselves and others. As women, we are often acutely aware of the impact money has on our relationships.

Though financial advisors suggest we just be rational in our dealings with money, this is rarely possible for most of us, as we attach a complex set of thoughts, beliefs, and feelings to money. I refer to this as our "inner money life." These beliefs and feelings are inherited from our culture, often reinforced by our parents, and continually augmented by our personal experiences with money. They influence how we handle—and don't handle—our money matters. They are our guiding principles, our personal money rules and laws.

This cluster of thoughts and feelings is largely outside our conscious awareness, so we often don't know what is driving our money behavior. Yet it affects every aspect of our lives, from the food we place in our grocery basket to the relationships we have with our friends and families; from how we view others as successful or lacking to our own sense of identity and self-worth. By becoming aware of our inner money life, and healing the parts of it that are getting in our way, we not only can understand how we feel about money and why we feel the ways we do, but we can also put our feelings about money to work for us in a positive way and prevent them from unconsciously pulling us in unwanted directions and derailing our best intentions.

EXPLORING EXPERIENCES OF MONEY

Emotional Currency is a guide to exploring your personal experiences of having, not having, making, not making, spending, saving, giving, investing, inheriting, and losing money. It is my hope that it will inspire you to see just how complex and rich your feelings about money actually are, and in the process, you will learn much that is new and eye-opening about yourself. It will teach you how to integrate your feelings into money matters. *Emotional Currency* will help you value the feminine approach to money and allow you to deal with money with your heart as well as your mind. It will expand your understanding of money from simply amounts and numbers to textured and nuanced stories that show how deeply our relationship to money can influence the people and things we love most in our lives.

Working with this book will not only breathe new life into your relationship with money, but also change your life for the better in the process. This is not about getting rich quick, but about enriching your life. You will learn how to make clear and conscious decisions that are appropriate to your current financial circumstances and what you value, and discover how a healthy relationship to money can improve your sense of self and your relationships with your family and friends. Finally, this book will assist you in finding the right place in your life for money—taking up neither too much nor too little space—and using money to enhance and support what you value in your life and in the world. Exploring your experiences with money will improve your relationship with money whether it is currently a source of big problems or of small anxiety.

BEYOND BASIC NEEDS

Eventually, I discovered what was true for me was also true for many other women: even when our basic needs are met, such as housing, food, medical care, transportation, and such, there are huge wells of confusion, pain, and distress in our relationship with money. Of course, not having enough money for basic living expenses presents very real and serious problems that cause much pain and suffering for far too many people, even in an affluent country like the United States. I do not underestimate the enormous difficulties created by a true lack of money, such as living in dangerous neighborhoods, going without medical care and insurance, lacking decent transportation, living paycheck to paycheck in low-wage jobs with little job security, lacking access to decent child care, being unable to leave abusive relationships, being unable to pay bills for essential services, and many other hardships. Living in poverty is extremely challenging and the way out of it is daunting.

But if we have enough to cover our basic needs, much of the money angst we experience stems from our inner money life, which can also be a source of difficulty and pain. Whether we scrub floors, teach children, program computers, perform surgeries, or do some other work to earn money or are handed it on a silver platter, money plays a significant psychological and emotional role in our lives and we react powerfully to it. Are you wondering if this is true for you? Then just consider how you would react if your best friend asked you to lend her a substantial sum of money. Or if you disagreed sorely with your partner over whether you can afford to take a vacation. Or if you didn't have the money to buy something your child needs. Or if you found you had been overcharged at the last store you visited or realized you had just scored a "steal of a deal." Our money dramas, both big and small, are often potent triggers for emotional reactions, thoughts, and associations.

OUR INNER MONEY LIFE

When I began to explore my inner money life, I discovered, much to my great surprise, that money had taken charge of my life in subtle ways. At the grocery store or at a restaurant, my choices were based on price, not on what I really wanted to eat. My entertainment decisions were similarly narrow: I would go to a concert or event only if it fell within the narrow price range that felt comfortable to me. I was incapable of splurging on one show even if I skipped another. I only bought clothes on sale or at thrift stores, and I planned vacations mostly to locations where I could stay with friends. My interest in attending classes, conferences, and lectures was all based on the cost, not the content.

This had all seemed normal to me, falling under the category of sound budgeting. Though I didn't have unlimited funds, I had enough money to eat an expensive entrée, go to a pricey concert, or buy a coat I really wanted. (Not to mention that from a purely financial perspective, buying what I wanted might well have translated into savings. For example, I would have been satisfied longer with the coat I loved than the one I bought because it was on sale and then dumped a year or so later.) From the outside, my life didn't appear to be consumed by money. Even I had no clue that money unconsciously underlay many of the decisions I made. Money was walking hand in hand with my fears about life.

The denial of my complex emotions around money had persisted through my writing a dissertation on women with inherited wealth, working as a psychotherapist for years, and being in my own personal psychotherapy. It was only after I began to present the research findings from my dissertation that I realized I hadn't given any thought to my own relationship to money. It struck me as remarkable that even though I'd asked the women I'd interviewed to explore money psychologically, it hadn't ever occurred to me to do the same. I clearly needed help to see below the surface of my own relationship to money. I searched for a psychotherapist who was sane about money. And finding one, I slowly uncovered how important money had been in my family growing up, in my parents' lives, and in my own life.

The next layer of my psychological denial about money was pierced through when I watched real estate prices escalate dramatically shortly after my husband and I had sold our house. When we put the house on the market, I had wanted to sell with such certainty that I told myself it didn't matter how much the house might later increase in value. But as home values climbed after we sold, I became flooded with feelings of greed and regret. On my daily walks, I obsessed about the worth of the homes I passed. Some days I imagined myself to be a homeless woman, wandering the streets in search of shelter even though, in fact, I had a roof over my head. My reality didn't offer any comfort at all.

I knew I had become crazed about money when every day, and even in nightmares, I was gripped by the feeling that in selling our house we'd made a horrendous financial decision from which we could never recover. It doesn't really matter exactly what broke through my denial; it could have been anything that touched the right nerve. I attended a group on writing personal essays and wrote exclusively about my experiences with money. And still later, I formed a group with two friends just to talk about money. After the first meeting, I felt so ashamed of having revealed too much about myself that I considered dropping out of the group. Nonetheless, when I went to the next meeting, I learned that my friends, too, had considered not returning because they also felt they had exposed too much. Talking about money made all of us feel so vulnerable that we knew we were onto something big!

It seems amazing to me now that for years I was convinced that money didn't matter to me, when in fact it was so central to my life and I was so full of emotional conflict and fear about it that I couldn't face it.

I realized that money, far from not mattering, was unconsciously driving most of my decisions and much of my behavior. I uncovered the sources of pain from my childhood and my attachment to money as security. I saw that I was gripped with fear that terrible things would happen to me if I didn't have money. It became clear why I subliminally worried that I would run out of money all of the time. And why I longed for a man to rescue me financially. Not only did money hold feelings of security, life, and death for me, but it also represented love, belonging, rejection, shame, and self-esteem. My overall feelings about money were so complicated, it was no wonder that I continually lost my way with it.

Uncovering the chaotic feelings underlying my relationship to money led to a gold mine of information about my family and me, stories that I tell as the book progresses. Seeing and feeling the knot of sticky emotions that money evoked in my life was uncomfortable, but it was a huge relief when I finally got that knot untangled. It transformed my relationship to money into something far richer than any spreadsheet or brokerage statement had ever done for me.

Updating my inner money life removed my anxiety about money and allowed me to appreciate and use well what money I had. It gave me a new sense of self-esteem and confidence in my own abilities. It allowed me to disengage from money as the main determinant of value in my life. The financial cost of things still had its place in my decision-making process, but so did other considerations. For example, the workshop that earlier I would have rejected taking because it was too expensive became an option when I took other elements into consideration: it was with a teacher I *admired*, was on a subject of great *interest*, had practical *usefulness, would inspire* me, and there was a good chance I would *learn* a lot.

Once I started to uncover my own inner money life, I became curious about the money lives of my clients. I began asking them questions about money and was astounded by the richness of our conversations and the unexpected places they would lead. Money proved an immediate avenue into how they saw themselves, the way they related to the world, and what they valued.

Out of a growing appreciation that others had similarly intense experiences with money, and little opportunity to focus on their unique relationships with it, I created and led Emotional Currency Workshops.

These day-long workshops for women were based on two essential elements of my own process of getting grounded emotionally with money: writing and talking about my inner money life.

In my years of leading Emotional Currency Workshops and talking with women both in and out of my psychotherapy practice, I have come to appreciate how difficult it is for us to value our inner money lives, especially given the taboo against talking about money. Often our conversations about money led to discovering important longings, passions, pains, vulnerabilities, and experiences in our lives. We were talking about money, but it was about so much more than just money. The workshops provided a deeply intimate way to get to know one another, and given the agreement to be open about our emotional money lives, we were eager to share our stories and learn from one another.

The biggest discovery I made in witnessing the sharing that took place in the workshops was to realize how dearly the taboo against talking about money has cost women. Not only have women been disenfranchised for generations from their financial lives, they have also been kept from a primary way they learn: from talking to one another. The taboo remains firmly in place even though we have made strides in the workplace, in having control over our own money, and in making decisions about managing it. In order to break out of our financial isolation, value our experiences as women with money, and explore the uncharted area of emotion and money, we need to talk with one another and share our stories.

WHAT THIS BOOK OFFERS YOU

Emotional Currency provides what our friendships and acquaintances haven't generally been able to: access to other women's experiences of money; the kinds of money dilemmas they face; the secrets they haven't shared even with their closest friends; and, finally, the solutions they found. These stories will give you a sense of what lies beneath our money facades.

Among the women you will meet is Jessie, the first person in her family to make enough money to set some aside in savings. As she accumulated some reserves, her relatives asked her for "loans" to help them get by, and she found herself unable to decline their frequent requests. And you'll meet Amy, who couldn't bear to spend money on anything special just for herself, as each purchase reminded her of her parents' old arguments about money, spoiling whatever pleasure she might receive from her new acquisition.

You'll hear, too, from Fran, who had fully supported herself for years and had no trouble keeping her spending under control until she married Tom and began to run up credit card debt. Though she promised him repeatedly that she would stop overspending, she couldn't. Unable to figure out why Fran wasn't able to contain her shopping, the couple were close to divorce. You'll also meet Amber, a chef who long dreamed of opening her own restaurant and faced numerous obstacles to actualize her dream.

The women in *Emotional Currency* face complicated situations. Rich or poor and everything in between, the women found the solutions to their dilemmas by looking within themselves. Their success at overcoming their difficulties with money—and knowing that the same opportunity could be available to a much wider range of women—is the reason I wrote this book. Men, too, who have long ignored their emotions about money, can benefit from this book. They can use it to come closer to understanding their own emotional responses to money as well those of the women in their lives.

Emotional Currency offers tools to help you learn how to listen to, value, and work with your direct experiences, thoughts, and feelings about money in your ordinary, daily life. I have found these tools to be very useful and employ them in my practice to help my clients create healthy, empowered relationships to money. Even if you doubt this is possible, I assure you that it can happen—I have witnessed it in my own life and the lives of the many other women with whom I've worked.

No book can address all the issues around money. For example, as important as poverty is, this book does not deal with the impact of poverty, including hunger, malnutrition, lack of medical care, and shorter life expectancy. These are all immense problems, individually and collectively, that require large scale political and societal solutions. Yet I believe the more we move our own feelings about money into the light, the more we can see and care about the effect of money on the lives of others. By exploring the inner, personal sides of money, we often become more engaged with the outer aspects of money, including its relationship to politics, spirituality, business, the natural world, the arts, and education. Shifting to a personal awareness allows us to place value not only on money, but also on other meaningful resources which can include our relationships with one another (those we know and those we don't in our global community) and the health and well-being of the planet and all its inhabitants.

It is clear to me that we need new solutions to the financial dilemmas that exist on every level of society. As women have control over more money, we approach a point in history when women's conceptions of money can begin to influence how the larger world perceives and deals with it. How money looks, feels, and operates would be very different if the contributions of both men and women—and the masculine and the feminine approaches to money—were equally valued. It's far from the total solution to the current economic climate of uncertainty, greed, and unethical dealmaking, but we desperately need the humanizing element of the feminine integrated into our economic thinking and solutions. For women to influence the face of money will require a movement of women dealing with each other in new ways, informed by a feminine ethic.

But for now, let's begin where we are, and work on having a healthier relationship to money. No matter what your relationship is currently like, I believe reading *Emotional Currency* will make it much better. Read it with an open mind and an open heart, and you will find new sources of strength, resilience, insight, and confidence.

❧

understanding
money

Welcome all your inner experiences of money.

Feelings of joy and fulfillment are no more or less valuable

than envy and shame. Let your reactions lead you to

a deeper place within yourself.

CHAPTER 1
....
Money as Emotional Currency

🌹

There was little money in my family as I was growing up, so in order to survive we all helped each other out. Now that I have extra money, and I'm the only one who does, I'm never able to say no to their requests for help, even when I want to. —JESSIE

ON THE SURFACE, our relationship to money appears straightforward and uncomplicated: either we have enough of it or we don't. But there are few subjects as emotionally charged, deeply personal, and culturally complex as money. Though the fields of economics, finance, and psychology have given little notice to inner money lives, for most of us, there is more to how money works than simply using it to make ends meet. In order to have a full relationship with it, we need to understand money as both tangible and symbolic as well as recognize our responses to it as both emotional and rational—we have to become good jugglers! This chapter will help you expand your awareness of the range of emotions money can evoke in you—and in all of us.

TO SHARE—OR NOT TO SHARE?

Jessie had worked her way up the career ladder in real estate. She found working hard and watching her savings grow very rewarding. When she first left home, she hadn't known why she had such a strong urge

13

to move across the country, but it later became clear to her that she had been trying to leave her family's poverty behind. Having more than enough money now not only made her feel more secure and competent, it was also a tangible sign of her distance from poverty.

She was the first in her family to have any savings, and her parents, two brothers, and a sister, all living marginally, continually asked her to bail them out of one crisis or another with requests for loans. Jessie always said yes to these requests as she had more than enough to pay for the car repair or the medication or to help cover the rent or kids' participation in sports activities. Everyone knew these weren't the kind of loans that would be paid back. And for years there had been nothing Jessie would rather do with her money than help her family out. But her feelings changed.

She shared in an Emotional Currency Workshop, "At some point, I began to feel resentful of the constant cries for help. I noticed that I was cringing each time the phone rang, dreading that it was yet another call for money. My relationships with my family had started to feel like they were all about the money. I didn't like feeling so obligated to give to them. I'm a frugal person, and I developed judgments about how they were spending the money I gave them. *My* money. So, for lots of reasons, I decided I needed to say no to at least some of the requests. But since making up my mind to say no six months ago, I haven't been able to say it even once. Now, on top of all these other feelings, I feel like a failure for not being able to do what I say I want to do."

Jessie was on a roller-coaster ride about her money. Happy to be sharing it at first, once she decided to assert her autonomy over her money, she felt guilty and conflicted about following through with that decision. As she explored why it had been impossible for her just to say no to her family's requests, Jessie discovered lots of contradictory feelings. "I resent feeling obligated to be the financial savior for my family," she said. "But on the other hand, I love being needed and able to help them out. We were always there for each other growing up, so it's very familiar to do whatever I can. Needing each other made us really close. I'm proud of what I've accomplished, but it comes with a lot of guilt for living far away from them as well as for making such good money. I must be afraid that I won't be able to bear the extra guilt that will come from my saying no."

This line of thinking led Jessie to realize that the money she gave her family members was in part an attempt to buy them off, to quiet their anger at her for having left them—both geographically and financially. And the checks also served to dispel her guilt. Talking it through in the workshop, she came to see her belief that if she didn't bail her family out she would be alone in the world—which she feared more than just about anything.

Not only did Jessie love her family very much and want to be close to them, she didn't think she could survive without them. So although she had thought she was just helping them, in fact she had also been protecting herself from their anger, her guilt, and her fear of losing them.

Seeing all these threads helped Jessie to untangle her emotional money knot. "I know, and need to reassure myself, that even though my siblings might well be mad at me for denying their requests, our relationships with each other go way beyond money. There may be some rocky times financially and emotionally, but perhaps something good can come of it as well. I know it will free me up to call and visit them more often—to once again want to be with them. I think I'll open a savings account for my nieces' and nephews' future, so if they choose to attend college, want to get training, or start a business, I will have the funds to help them out."

WHAT'S THE PROBLEM?

How many of us have decided to treat money differently: buy less of something, give more to charity, save more, or even spend more? Like Jessie, we think there is something wrong with us if our money behavior isn't in line with what we decide it should be. But dealing with money is rarely easy. As in Jessie's case, much of the time money isn't the problem or the dilemma—it's our feelings about money that create the problem. And these feelings often pull us in several directions, as they did Jessie, without our being aware of the origin of our contradictory desires.

Once we have enough money to meet our basic needs, money's influence over us comes mainly from what it symbolizes or represents for us. When asked what it symbolizes, Americans often answer with one word: power. That's true enough for some, especially for men. Yet for most women, and some men, money represents a mixture of many things, including guilt, pain, danger, and fear as well as love, self-worth, nurturance, and security.

Perhaps it would be more appropriate to use the plural "monies" to convey that money is never any single idea, exchange, meaning, feeling, or concept—either in the world at large or within ourselves. We each have a unique inner money life. Within each of us are layer upon layer of feelings, memories, meanings, and associations involving money. These meanings and feelings can change depending on the moment, the context, the people involved, our roles, our ages, our phases of life, economic conditions, or our bank balance. New financial landscapes evoke even more bewildering emotions when we divorce, marry, become widowed, inherit, lose our job, become the breadwinner, have a baby, retire, or the economy tanks. The multiple shifts in meaning that money carries for us are largely outside our awareness.

THE POWER OF FEELINGS

One of the dimensions that contributes to each of us being distinctly individual is how we experience emotions. What sorrow feels like to me may well be different than what it feels like to you. In addition, the intensity and duration of feelings vary. Feelings always come and go, but for some of us, some feelings may stick around only for a few minutes, while for others our emotions might last for days, months, or years.

In both my personal and professional life, I use the terms *emotion* and *feeling* interchangeably and place them, along with thought, at the center of our experience. I understand them to be spontaneous, subjective reactions that we cannot consciously will. Not only can we not will them, we are not even aware of most of our emotional reactions until we put some effort into paying attention to them. Once we are familiar with an emotional response, we are able to identify it more easily when it occurs again.

Many people differentiate between emotion and feelings, thinking of emotion as tied to a physiological reaction or bodily sensation, as in "feeling it in my gut," or "having a broken heart," or racing pulses or sluggishness. In that way of thinking, feelings are what come from our emotions, from these visceral responses. Others see emotions as intense forms of feeling that take over our attention, with feelings being more subtle and fluid.

In some circles, feelings have a bad reputation. They are seen as untrustworthy. But the valuable information that feelings offer us is lost and we make poorer choices—in this case, poorer financial choices—when we don't give them attention. In order to have the whole picture, we need to know when we are feeling ashamed and envious, exuberant and fearless, or concerned and cautious about a money decision. Not only do we need to consider how our feelings might be influencing our thinking, but our feelings are showing us something significant about how we are experiencing or dealing with money. Feelings talk to us of values, relationships, desires, and fears. And they offer the only path for healing our wounds from our painful experiences and emotions involving money.

Our inner money life needs attention just like other parts of our emotional lives. To some extent, all of us have learned to cope with our feelings by blocking them, pushing them away, denying them, and ignoring them. And most of us learned that emotions were problems, that we'd be better without them in our lives. Actually, problems arise not because we have emotions, but because we don't attend to them. If we see emotions as somehow getting in our way, something like an irritating insect buzzing around our face, we will cut them off and try to ignore them.

But feelings that aren't acknowledged, understood, and digested don't disappear. They continue to play an active role in our lives, just outside of our awareness, and can cause us problems. They become unseen influences that affect—some would even say control—our behavior. Chronic jealousy, envy, discontentment, and shame about money are all signs of a blocked, unexamined, and unhealed money life. So is chronic overspending, as well as greed, hoarding, and obsessions with savings and investments. We can use money to act out feelings we can't acknowledge or express in other ways. Thus, how we behave with money can illuminate how we are feeling.

Emotions need to be noticed and given attention. It may sound funny, but we need to have a relationship with our feelings. For example, grief is an emotion we tend to push away, thinking we should get over it and get on with our lives. But when we prematurely push it aside, be it grief from the death of a parent or a spouse or the loss of income from an illness, it will masterfully express itself in other ways. Suppressed grief can take the form, in terms of our money lives, of not paying bills, overspending, or impulsivity with major financial decisions. Another example is pushing away our money anxieties which can encourage other behaviors that block emotions, such as substance abuse and compulsive eating, exercise, and work.

With attention, we can learn to recognize our feelings as they surface. Sometimes we merely need to notice them and let them pass. Other times we need to delve into them further, to explore and understand them. What are they telling us about ourselves? About others? Is there some action we need to take in response to them?

So how do you get to know your emotions or feelings about money? Your investigation can be stimulated by any number of things: an exchange, a problem, a question, an incident, an observation, a memory, a situation, or a thought involving money. You can focus on something from your past or something as it is happening. I find that it can sometimes be too general and difficult to focus directly on money in the past, especially if the experiences carry a lot of emotional weight. One way to get your emotional juices flowing about money is to go about your daily life and see what grabs you. The present offers immediate content and feelings to work with as well as all the accompanying associations to past experiences. For instance, realizing you've just ordered the least expensive item on the menu rather than one of the pricier entrées that you really wanted, you can become aware of what you are feeling, perhaps a sense of deprivation and frustration. Or watching how freely you spend money on shoes brings up associations to your mother's shoe indulgences and a feeling of being cared for. Or noticing that you stay upset with yourself for days for having gotten a ticket when you pushed your luck with the parking meter which reminds you of your anger in response to your ex telling you that you had no appreciation of the value of a dollar. Each specific situation is a starting point for exploring your feelings and where they come from.

When exploring your feelings, don't settle for what is familiar, habitual, or your family's "party line." One helpful approach to uncovering your reactions and feelings about money is to shake up some of the patterns you have developed, even taking a more playful attitude with money, and watch what arises within you. These seemingly superficial shifts in habit can lead to big insights. Here are some suggestions you might try:

- If you usually put most of your purchases on a credit card or pay with a debit card, try spending only cash for a month.
- Buy something inexpensive and then buy something expensive.
- If you usually try to buy things on sale, pay full price. And vice versa.
- If you generally go dutch when out with a friend, pay for your friend's dinner or movie next time.
- Show a friend the contents of your wallet.
- Bargain with a shopkeeper about the price of something.
- Don't buy anything for a week.

Any of these experiences will put you in touch with your feelings about money. The more experiences you try, the more feelings you will uncover, now that you're watching for them.

Feelings are excellent vehicles for taking us into our past. Sometimes feelings lead us to recall important lessons and experiences that are helpful and nourishing to our current situation. They also help us to revisit events that are still causing us conflict and confusion and that need more attention. We can look again at these undigested feelings, bringing the new perspectives and insights we've gained through living our lives, and make new sense of our feelings. Visiting the past these ways is not about living in the past—but rather integrating what it taught us so we can loosen its grip over us and not continually relive and recreate it. The goal is to discriminate and liberate our present experience from the past, so we can more fully live in the present and make the best choices and decisions for the future.

Money is somewhat mysterious, so no matter how much you know about it, there will be new things to discover. Curiosity is the best vantage point for seeing emotional truth. There are no wrong emotions—we feel what we feel. We can work with our emotions and, by seeing, understanding, and digesting them, we can often transform how we relate to them and whatever is stimulating them—in this case, money. I can't emphasize enough that sitting in judgment about yourself doesn't serve you in any way. That doesn't mean you have to like everything about your emotions; you just need to accept them and begin to understand and appreciate why you feel the way you do.

Luckily there is no lack of opportunity to observe ourselves and our money behavior. Most of our lives hold countless dramas and incidents relating to money that we may have forgotten or may never have told anyone or whose meaning we haven't yet fully appreciated. Sometimes even a small money exchange can be revealing, leading us to a fruitful exploration of unexamined emotional reactions to money.

For example, Angela's experience: "As I was loading my groceries into the car recently, I discovered that I had been charged $7.29 a pound for potatoes that had been marked 59 cents. I was tired, I wanted to go home, but I wasn't going to let them get away with overcharging me. As I went through the process of getting a refund, I noticed how irritated and angry I was. I was reacting as if I was getting ripped off even though it was one of my favorite stores, I knew well it was an unintentional error, and that I couldn't recall ever being overcharged in all the years I'd shopped there. The intensity of my reaction and my inability to hold the context of the situation and consider all my positive feelings about the store alerted me to there being something I needed to explore in my feelings about being ripped off."

A note of caution here: some people are continually flooded and overwhelmed by emotion. You will know if you fall into this category. If this description fits you, your task here is to work toward discerning which feelings are most important for you to focus on. And I suggest you do the work recommended in this book, but with the emphasis on observation and making intellectual connections rather than arousing more feeling.

Exercise: Words That Describe Money

Here's an exercise to help you get a sense of the scope of your feelings about money. Sit down and close your eyes for a moment. Place your attention on money and think about any words that you associate with it. They can be qualities, feelings, objects, experiences, meanings, nouns, verbs, and adverbs. Once the words begin flowing, write them down in a blank journal (which you'll need for your money memoir in the next chapter) or on a sheet of paper.

I suggest you give yourself at least ten minutes for this exercise. When you feel your word list is complete, take a look at the following compilation, or master list. Or wait awhile before looking at the list and allow additional words to percolate over the course of reading this book.

The following list was compiled from word lists shared by women participating in my workshops. Don't be concerned by the length or brevity of your list, and feel free to add any words that resonate for you. And though the list is long, some of your choices may not be included.

Abandonment	Anxiety	Betrayal
Abundance	Appreciation	Bewildering
Abuse	Approval	Bipolar
Acceptance	Argument	Blame
Access	Arrogance	Boring
Accommodation	Attention	Bribe
Accountable	Authority	Budget
Accounting	Autonomy	Burden
Achievement	Avariciousness	Buying
Addiction	Aversion	Calculating
Adulthood	Avoidance	Callousness
Advancement	Award	Camaraderie
Adventure	Bailout	Care
Afford	Balance	Careless
Agitating	Bankruptcy	Caring
Alienating	Bargain	Catastrophe
Allowance	Beauty	Chaos
Ancestors	Belonging	Charity
Anger	Benefit	Cheap

Cheating

Child care

Choice

Cinderella

Class

Clout

Cocoon

Codependent

Cold

Coldhearted

Comfort

Compassion

Compensation

Competence

Competition

Compliant

Complicated

Complication

Compromise

Compulsion

Confidence

Confidential

Conflict

Confusion

Conserve

Contentment

Control

Corrupt

Counterfeit

Crass

Crazy

Creativity

Credit

Cruelty

Damaging

Dangerous

Death

Debt

Decay

Deception

Defining

Degrading

Delight

Demonic

Denial

Dependence

Depreciation

Depression

Deprivation

Deserving

Desire

Desperation

Destiny

Destitute

Destruction

Devastation

Differentiation

Difficult

Difficulties

Dirty

Disappointed

Discomfort

Discord

Disruption

Distress

Distrust

Disturbing

Divisive

Divorce

Dominance

Doubt

Down

Dread

Dream

Dysfunctional

Earning

Economical

Education

Elusive

Embarrassment

Empty

Encourage

Energy

Enjoyment

Enmeshment

Enough

Enslavement

Entitlement

Envy

Equality

Errors

Escape

Esteem

Etiquette

Evil

Excellence

Excess

Excitement

Exclusion

Expansion

Experiences

Extravagant

Exuberance

Failure

Fairness

Faith	Hate	Interconnection
Fake	Headache	Interest
False	Health	Intimidated
Fantasy	Health care	Intoxicating
Fate	Help	Investment
Father	Helpless	Isolating
Favoritism	Hidden	Jealousy
Fear	Hierarchy	Joy
Flexibility	High	Judgment
Food	Hoarding	Justice
Fortune	Home	Kindness
Freedom	Honesty	Lack
Fret	Hope	Lack of control
Frightening	Humiliation	Leisure
Frugality	Hunger	Lessons
Fulfillment	Hurt	Liberation
Fun	Illness	Lies
Future	Illusion	Life
Gain	Imagination	Life force
Gamble	Impulsive	Like
Game	Inadequate	Lineage
Generosity	Inclusion	Litigation
Gift	Incompetence	Loaded
Giving	Indebtedness	Loathing
Glorified	Independence	Longing
Gold digger	Indulgence	Loneliness
Good	Inept	Loss
Gratification	Inferior	Love
Gratitude	Inflation	Low
Greed	Inheritance	Luck
Grief	Insanity	Luxury
Growth	Insecurity	Lying
Guilt	Insomnia	Managing
Happiness	Instability	Manic
Harm	Insufficient	Manipulation

Martyrdom	Occupation	Privilege
Mask	Okay	Prize
Masochism	Old	Problems
Mathematical	Opportunity	Promiscuous
Maturity	Oppression	Promise
Mean	Options	Property
Meaning	Order	Protection
Means	Ostrich	Punishment
Measure	Out of control	Quality
Menacing	Overwhelm	Rage
Metaphor	Owning	Reality
Miserly	Pain	Receiving
Misery	Panic	Regret
Misfortune	Paralysis	Rejection
Misrepresentation	Paranoia	Relationship
Mistakes	Partnership	Relief
Mistrust	Patriarchy	Repetition
Modest	Patterns	Rescue
Morass	Perplexing	Resentment
Mother	Philanthropy	Resiliency
Motivation	Pleasure	Resource
Mutuality	Plenty	Resourceful
Mystery	Poison	Responsibility
Mystification	Polarization	Respect
Necessity	Positive	Restraint
Need	Possibility	Retirement
Negativity	Potential	Reward
Negotiate	Poverty	Risk
Net	Power	Roll of the dice
Nobility	Powerless	Romance
Nurturance	Power struggle	Roots
Nutrition	Preoccupation	Ruin
Obligation	Pride	Sacrifice
Obsession	Princess	Sad
Obstruction	Prioritizing	Sadism

Safety	Spendthrift	Tenuous
Satisfaction	Spirit	Terror
Save	Spoiled	Things
Scarcity	Stability	Thinking
Scary	Starvation	Thrifty
Secrecy	Stature	Tight
Security	Status	Time
Seductive	Stealing	Tiring
Self-betrayal	Stewardship	Toxic
Self-denial	Stimulating	Trade-off
Self-destructive	Stingy	Transformation
Self-esteem	Strength	Trapped
Self-indulgent	Stress	Traumatic
Selfish	Strings	Trickery
Self-reliance	Struggle	Trust
Self-righteous	Style	Turned on
Self-soothing	Submission	Uncertain
Self-sufficiency	Success	Uncomfortable
Self-worth	Suffering	Underachieve
Selling out	Sufficiency	Undermining
Servitude	Suffocating	Undeserving
Sex	Sugar Daddy	Unequal
Sexy	Superiority	Unfair
Shame	Superstition	Unjust
Share	Support	Unknown
Shelter	Survival	Up
Shock	Suspect	Uprooted
Shopping	Suspicious	Uptight
Shoulds	Sustainability	Vacations
Show-off	Taboo	Value
Siblings	Taxes	Values
Sleeplessness	Taxing	Vanity
Sophistication	Tedious	Vice
Sorrow	Temptation	Victim
Space	Tension	Vilified

Vindictive	Wealth	Workaholic
Vulnerable	Well-being	Worry
Want	Withholding	Worth
Wasteful	Work	Worthless

You may have been surprised by the feelings and memories evoked by this exercise. Keep the reality of those feelings in mind as we consider another reality—one that may seem at odds with what you just experienced in the exercise.

THE FINANCIAL VIEW

What I call the financial view of money dominates American culture, with money being thought of simply as a measure of value, a medium of exchange, and a means of storing wealth. This view concerns itself with rational analysis, investment, the bottom line, wealth accumulation, interest, debt, taxes, profit, and loss. An impersonal view put forth by economists and financial experts, money is seen as an object that can—indeed, must—be dealt with rationally and logically. When we think of money only as an object, separate and apart from us, it is reasonable to view it solely in these black-and-white terms, as gain or loss, enough or not enough, spend or save—either you have it or you don't.

Centuries of Western thought have placed trust in reason and found emotion to be unreliable. Moreover, financial experts advise us that blending emotion and money is a recipe for disaster—that taking our feelings into account will blind us to the hard-and-fast realities of how money works in the world. Thus, the rational science of economics is esteemed while our subjective, emotional experience of money has been dismissed as, at best, irrelevant and, at worst, dangerous to sound money practices.

The rational approach to money certainly has its place, but if dealing with money was simply a rational act and if a dollar was just a dollar, we wouldn't worry so much about it, and we certainly wouldn't spend more money than we have. Obviously, it's more complicated than that, and the rational approach is insufficient for truly understanding our relationship to money. We obsess, lie, and act secretively about our finances. Most of us never feel we have enough money. We have credit card and home equity debt. We hoard money at times and splurge impulsively at others. We cheat and manipulate to get money. And we fight with family members, overtly and covertly, over finances.

All we have to do is read the business section of a daily newspaper to see convoluted dramas of greed, betrayal, and dishonesty involving money. In our own lives and the lives of friends and family, we witness confusion, fear, pain, strength, love, creativity, and generosity as we and they face financial uncertainties as well as successes. Not only can't many of us turn off our "feeling-full" reactions to money, perhaps we don't need to.

Working as an accountant, Rachel discovered the surprising degree to which money was emotional. After divorcing, she needed to find a way to support herself and her son. She explained, "I'd always been good with numbers and decided to become an accountant after I realized that the barriers I felt as a woman in dealing with money weren't carved in stone as I had imagined. I grew up thinking that finance and money belong to a secret society that only males were allowed into. It was like the orthodox synagogue I grew up in, where the women were upstairs and only the men were allowed to be near the Torah. I realized that money, like Jewish prayer, wasn't all that secret, I just had to educate myself about it."

As Rachel became more competent in accounting, she began to notice that all of her clients, men as well as women, were emotional in their meetings with her. She observed universal feelings of shame about how they were handling their financial affairs, whether for how much money they had or the condition of their record keeping. Several clients were humiliated by bringing her their year's receipts in a shoe box, unable to sort through them on their own. Other clients were embarrassed either by how much they'd earned or how much they'd spent. Another client, a woman who had inherited five million dollars, was ashamed that she still worried that she didn't have enough money. Rachel noticed the conversations she began to have with her clients about their feelings actually brought improvement to how they handled their money matters. And perhaps most importantly, the conversations led to her clients' clarifying who and what they valued in their lives, enabling them to make better decisions about money. Rachel didn't start off intending to integrate feeling into her approach to working with her clients, but she discovered that doing so made for better accounting.

It is challenging to look at money in its emotional complexity in a culture like ours that sees money as a tangible object to be managed in rational, black-and-white terms and whose predominant message is to blindly and unthinkingly spend, spend, spend. Our economy needs us to not think too much about money. However, far from being irrelevant or dangerous, our feelings about money are informative, instructive, enlightening, empowering—and influential.

Further, some of us cannot begin to see money financially until we have sorted through our emotional responses to it. It's not a matter of merely pushing our feelings aside, because they can't be dismissed so easily. We need to work with the knot of emotions to untangle it, figure out what we feel and why we feel it. Some of our feelings can enliven and animate our financial relationship to money, others can obstruct it. It's the ones that obstruct and cause us money problems that we need to heal.

TWO SIDES OF THE COIN

Just as you can now see from doing the previous excerise on page 21, there is no one list of words that encompasses everything that money means to each of us, there is also no right way to think—or feel—about money. The list graphically shows that money has an amazing capacity to take on many symbolic and emotional meanings. And though they may not seem as real as the dollar bills we touch every day, these nontangible forms are not only real, but hold a powerful place in our psyches and lives.

Because money represents so many different things for each of us, it's easy to get confused about what money can and cannot buy. The confusion is not just personal. It's actually quite difficult to be emotionally balanced about money in our culture. It can be done—but it takes the kind of conscious effort described in this book. And because money is so influential and omnipresent in our lives, we are well advised to spend the time to understand it from both the inside—being our personal, inner money realities—and the outside—being our financial realities, and the external economic conditions and cultural forces.

Beyond the tangible and concrete forms of money, what we think of as its reality is something that we have learned from our culture and our experiences. Some of what we've learned and inherited may be a good fit with our desires, psychology, and values. But some of it may be disabling or destructive to us. We each have the task to see what's true for us about money in our life—our current inner money life—and then make some choices about what we want to keep as ours, what we need to discard, and what we could add.

To have a full relationship to money, we must value both its concrete and symbolic sides and recognize that there is constant flow back and forth between the two. One moment the $20 bill in my hand is just a paper bill used to go to the movies, and the next moment it's the means for expressing my gratitude to a friend, trying to buy my daughter's love, or a way to add my support to a cause or project in which I believe.

On one side of the coin for most of us, money holds a compelling array of feelings, many of them slippery and contradictory. These include guilt, conflict, regret, greed, grief, denial, and fear. We can't seem to hold on to money. Our worries about it keep us up at night. We are ashamed of having too much. We are ashamed of having too little. We feel like we never have enough. We argue with our partners about it. We avoid dealing with money matters. We're angry at ourselves for either buying or selling whatever we've bought or sold. We give money to a charity, loan it to a friend, or use it for a splurge and immediately regret it. We can't figure out if we have enough to pay next month's bills, take a vacation, or retire.

On the other side of the coin, money can bring feelings of success, confidence, relief, joy, satisfaction, empowerment, and connection. We get paid a bonus and get something we really needed or wanted. We have extra money and make a donation to a cause we support. We take care of others. Something needs repair and we are able to fix it without worrying where the money will come from. We leave our unhappy marriage because we have our own income. We spend our money on experiences that enrich us. We pay down our credit card bills or add to our savings.

For some women, and even more men, money doesn't carry so much emotion—money is just money. This is an essential viewpoint for women who work in some aspect of finance handling other peoples' money. Deborah, a woman who had started several investment companies, said she was attracted to the intellectual stimulation of investing, to the "limitless" nature of the thinking it demanded. Making money was not the draw for her, rather she loved that finance required her to research constantly changing topics within economics, history, business, and global affairs.

Deborah can now see that what led her to work in banking and investments had something to do with her father who, though working class, followed the market with passion and taught her the vocabulary of investing from an early age. In finance, she was able to hold her own in the face of male authority. It was being really good at what she did that brought her pleasure, as well as being equally successful, if not more succesful, than men in the male world of finance. Whatever the emotional undercurrents in her need to excel in the world of finance, she told me that money was not emotional and that her dealings with it didn't have any emotional baggage.

Another woman in the financial field, Stephanie, a wealth advisor for a major brokerage firm, agreed that money is just money to her, though it wasn't always that way. She told me, "In my first marriage my husband did not trust me financially, so he took away my ATM card and check writing privileges and would only give me a bit of cash every week to get by. I started believing that I was bad with money.

"I think I was drawn to this industry because the numbers are the numbers. So if I bring in a million dollars in revenue and the guy next to me brings in a million dollars, we make the same amount of money. It's a complete meritocracy. In a world where women continually work harder for less pay, this feels like liberation. That's not to say that there isn't a big ol' boys club that we'll never be invited into, but that as long as we can find our way around it, we can be successful."

And Marissa, a stockbroker, said, "Mood management is crucial to portfolio management. The markets move on greed and fear and my greatest challenge has always been to keep myself on a calm, analytic, skeptical, if not cynical, footing."

Deborah, Stephanie, and Marissa's ways of thinking may be very different from your own. They have grown comfortable with the responsibility of managing large quantities of other people's money because they have the ability to see money simply as money, without the accompanying layers of association, emotion, and relationship. This view of money confirms the saying, attributed to Sigmund Freud (albeit in a different context), "Sometimes a cigar is just a cigar." It is good for all of us to have the ability to see money this way, some of the time.

Money also confirms the ideas, inherent in Freud's statement but generally overlooked regarding money, that sometimes a cigar is *not* just a cigar—meaning that money is open to a great deal of personal interpretation. Given the wide diversity among us—who we are, where we are in our lives, and what has brought us to this point—we will inevitably have many variations in our ways with money.

I've included many stories in this book of women from a wide range of circumstances and stories of my own as well. All the stories I share are true, though for confidentiality, the names and identifying details have all been changed. In some cases, several stories are merged into one.

HOW MONEY OPERATES

Before we explore the realities of money in your own life and in the lives of other women, consider the following ways money operates dynamically in American culture. Many of these topics will be discussed more fully in the rest of the book. For now, use the questions here to begin to think about money in your life. These questions, like all the questions in the book, don't lend themselves to yes or no answers, but rather are meant to encourage you to contemplate your relationship to money. Let the questions that interest you stimulate your thoughts. You may want to jot some notes in your journal as you read through them.

Money carries our anxiety about survival. We need money to provide for our basic physical needs: food, shelter, and clothing. It is hard to imagine our survival apart from money. Money carries a current of fear and insecurity as well as of safety and security. We are uncomfortable with how vulnerable we are to the social, economic, physical, and personal changes that threaten our financial well-being. Consider the following:

- Do you ever worry about not having enough money for your basic needs?
- If so, what triggers your fears?
- What do you imagine would happen to you?
- Have you lived through periods in your life when you or your family didn't have enough money for food, clothing, and shelter? Or when you worried you wouldn't have enough?
- If so, what was that like for you?
- How does it effect you now?

Money is an agent of transformation. People do remarkable things with money. Money can be transformed into something it is not—an endless number of objects, entities, desires, and experiences. As it flows from one hand to the next, money turns into something different with each exchange. Money also enables us to do things that transform ourselves, others, and our environment. Ask yourself:

- What is the money in your wallet or your bank account going to transform into today or in the near future?
- What experiences did money enable you to have recently?
- Have you used money to transform your self, home, neighborhood, community, or the world? In what ways?

Money is constantly in motion. Money passes from hand to hand and is never still for long. It changes value from moment to moment, both in terms of what it can buy and how much of it we have. We think we have X amount of dollars, then the stock market drops, a hurricane hits, or the services we provide become obsolete or less desired. Some of the fear we have about money comes from this constant change, a wildness that, in many ways, is outside of our control. Think about:

- Are there things about money always changing and being unpredictable that you like?

- What about its wild and uncontrollable nature scares you?

Money is a measure of value. Money is the only standard measure of value we have. Money homogenizes value and enables the comparison of quantitative differences such as the value of a house or a gallon of gas. It provides the marketplace with an enormously useful single scale. It has also become a method of valuing human worth in our culture. Our salaries, income, and assets are supposedly indicators of our value. Money is woven into our sense of self and self-worth, confusing human worth with monetary worth. Few of us escape learning to measure the worth of people by money, ourselves included. Reducing so much to so little, as money does so well, turns out to be an equally profound limitation when comparing qualitatively different experiences or, say, human beings. It is difficult to measure human qualities such as integrity, generosity, creativity, selfishness, or sadism with money. Until remarkably recently, and still true in many places, a woman's economic value came exclusively through the status and standing of her family and husband. Ask yourself:

- How is money tied to your self-esteem?
- How does how much you earn influence your sense of own value in the world?
- How does the appearance of someone having or not having money affect how you see them?

Money is both rational and emotional. The economic model of money is a rational model, concerned with a statistical and material approach. But our dealings with money can also be nonrational, emotional, wild, and symbolic. In order to have a *whole* relationship to money as individuals and as a culture, we need to include both rational and nonrational perspectives. Consider:

- Off the top of your head, in what three ways do you deal with money rationally (such as balancing your checkbook or creating a budget)?

33

- In what three ways do you deal with money emotionally (such as impulse gifts for a friend or reacting to a friend's subtle bragging about going on an expensive vacation)?

Money has everything to do with relationships. At its heart, it is based in relationship, for it is an agreement with others that worthless pieces of paper, metal, shell, and whatever else passes for money have value. We use it to exchange goods and services and to make other kinds of economic transactions with one another. Common or reciprocal monetary systems promote interaction and understanding between people. Ask yourself:

- Do you have relationships that have developed through money exchanges, perhaps with people who pay you for your services or products, or people whom you pay?
- In what ways have these relationships contributed to your life?

Money shows us our need for one another. From the moment of birth, we rely on others for our survival. One of the forms this dependency takes throughout our lives is money—receiving pay for our labors, earning money through investments, or being supported. Money doesn't fall from the sky; it comes to us from other people. There is no such thing as pure economic independence; financially, we are irrevocably intertwined and interdependent. Ask yourself:

- What relationships do you have that involve money?
- How does money intertwine with them?
- In what ways does it enhance those relationships?
- In what ways does it create problems?
- Whom do you depend on for money?
- Who depends upon you?

Money connects us to others. Money forms a bridge between us and others. Gifts and loans of money between family and friends are a sign of connection. Even a simple "Let me pick up the lunch check today" forms a connection. Philanthropy and charity are expressions of a connection with unknown people. Monetary exchanges often have social components to them, whether they occur at the corner small store, at a big box store, or on the phone. We may choose to spend our money in certain places because we are concerned for the well-being of the owner or employees. Ask yourself:

- Which money exchanges have made you feel closer to other people?
- With whom and in what ways?

Money can distance us from others. When introduced into relationships, money can sometimes dominate interactions, making us relate in more impersonal and less caring ways. It can introduce conflict between people. Withholding money can create distance. How many times have we heard about business partners or family members who have stopped talking to one another over disagreements or betrayals centering on money? Those in economic difficulties often do not let even their close friends know of their worries. And as the middle class shrinks and the gap between the upper and lower classes grows, those at either end of the spectrum increasingly inhabit strikingly different realities that most of us are unable, unwilling, or ignorant of how to bridge. Consider:

- Have you experienced conflicts with others over money that have caused distance?
- Which money exchanges have made you feel distant from someone?
- From whom and in what ways?
- Have you felt isolated because of your financial situation?

Money can be a motivator. People do remarkable things for money. Beneficial things, as well as dangerous and immoral things, happen because of money. It is a tangible form of human energy and time. If it weren't for the need for money, some of us would not have continued to show up at our jobs, finished school, or done things that helped us to develop all sorts of abilities and understandings of ourselves and the world. Questions about money as a motivator:

- What have you done for money that you otherwise would not have taken on?
- Were there ways this benefited you?
- Were there ways this was harmful?
- Are there experiences you have had or skills that you have learned because of a need or desire for money?
- Does doing something for money change your relationship to the activity?
- Has the introduction of money into something you are doing changed how you felt about that activity?
- Was money ever used to get you to do certain things or behave in certain ways when you were growing up?

Money can affect our sense of our place in the world. Having or not having money not only influences whether we have a literal home, but can also determine whether we have access to opportunities to work, make money, and contribute to the world. It can empower us psychologically to feel substantial and significant that feel we belong or disempower us to feel small and invisible and that there is no place for us. Where we see ourselves on this continuum may shift with our asset balance. Our wealth or lack of it can impact whether others believe in our abilities and provide us with chances to prove ourselves or judge us as worthless and dismiss us. Ask yourself:

- How does your financial status influence the way you feel about your current place in the world?
- When you were growing up, how did your family's financial status influence how you saw your place in the world?
- At what times has money made you feel special or opened doors for you?
- At what times has money made you feel disregarded or closed doors for you?
- How do you feel toward homeless people?
- How do you feel toward people in positions of wealth and power?

- Can you describe your reactions to specific people in both these categories of wealth?

Our personal monetary exchanges contain messages about who we are, how we see ourselves, and how others see us. Although we rarely speak of money, money is always talking—between spouses, partners, colleagues, bosses, children and parents, siblings, friends, acquaintances, customers and proprietors, and even strangers. We use money to communicate many things to others. We can feel valued, included, and respected, or rejected, punished, and marginalized through our financial dealings. As adults, we might feel neglected when our parents expect that we pay for lunch, or we might feel respected for picking up the tab. We could feel cheated by how much the shoe-repair person charged us, or favored if we were given a special deal. We might take pride in our bonus at work or feel devalued in comparison to what a coworker received. Consider:

- When did you feel neglected or undervalued by how someone treated you in a financial transaction?
- When did you feel valued by how someone treated you in a financial transaction?
- Who are a few of the people in your life that you sense treat you differently based on how much money you have or don't have?
- How does that feel to you?

Our personal monetary exchanges affect the quality of our lives and of our communities and the planet. Saving money when we spend is a source of pride and pleasure in our culture, one that the commercial world exploits with its constant promise of "if you spend now, you'll save more later!" As shoppers, most of us are conditioned to look for the best possible deal and to feel foolish if we pay full price. Though it is extremely difficult, and often impossible, to rationalize passing up immediate savings, it is good to realize that they may actually contain hidden costs. The loss of small retail businesses and manufacturing companies have resulted in job losses, substantially less money circulating locally and nationally, and a reduction in tax revenue. The consolidation of purchases and the pressure for the cheapest goods impact what gets produced and who produces it. Ethical labor and environmental practices generally cost more.

It's extremely hard not to just consider our own self-interest when purchasing goods online or in big box stores. For example, buying a book online will likely save quite a few dollars on each book purchased. These savings make it hard to care that it costs our city, county, and state governments the sales taxes that help support local schools, roadways, and emergency services. And hard to think about the loss of jobs provided by the independent bookseller and those who sell books and other items to the booksellers, as well as the loss of the goods and services that the bookstore purchases locally. And hard to consider that the consolidation of book sales online greatly influences what gets published and publicized. Generally, most of us don't realize the impact of our choices until the independent bookstore closes and we have no place to browse for books or hear authors speak. Or we can no longer find the kind of pen we've used for years because it wasn't a pen the big stores carry and so it disappears along with the small stationary stores. Each category of small business has a similar story—that as consumers we primarily look at our wallets and give little mind to the people involved, ethical practices, or supporting small businesses and producers. Consider:

- Does it matter to you where you buy things, or are cost and convenience the only determining factors?
- Have you noticed any change in the quality of your life or the life of your community as small retailers have gone out of business?
- Have you, or anyone you know, been impacted by the loss of Main Street U.S.A. shopping or "Made in the U.S.A." manufacturing?
- In what ways?
- Do you know where your clothing, cell phone, computer, bread, meat, and vegetables are produced or grown?

There's lots of complexity to money in our lives. I hope you are beginning to get a sense of how impossible it is to pin money down because it takes so many varied forms and is constantly changing, both in how we relate to it and in the larger world. You'll find by the time you reach the end of this book, money won't seem so slippery, as you learn to contain and direct its influence in your life. In the next chapter, you will begin to explore your own personal relationship to money through your money memoir.

Know that you are not alone.

Others have financial challenges—just like you.

There is no ideal way of looking at or

dealing with money. Finding your own way in

the present requires understanding your past.

CHAPTER 2

Writing Your Money Memoir

❧

My mother's wallet was always open to me. I could take whatever I wanted. But I never touched the bills in my father's money clip. —KATE

W E TALK ABOUT THE PAST with our friends: who we loved, what we've done, when we were successful, where we worked, and how we were hurt. We talk about the present: who we love, what confuses us, when we're happy, where we want to go, and how we are having difficulty. We seamlessly weave parts of our stories about nearly everything into our conversations. It's rare, however, that we talk much about money, beyond our latest shopping bargain. It's hard to talk about money! Consequently, we often don't know much about even our own history with money. A money memoir offers a way to rediscover our experiences.

A money memoir is your personal history and present life involving money, with a focus on pivotal events, experiences, exchanges, and people. It is a simple, yet powerful tool for remembering, understanding, healing, and changing your relationship to money.

Of all the forms of money work I've done, writing my money memoir was the most helpful in coming to understand deeply my relationship to money. No longer writing for school—and without anyone judging what or how I was writing—I was stunned to discover how revealing and therapeutic writing could be. Writing helped me remember long-forgotten incidents and see them with new insight and perspective.

Writing about small incidents illuminated big feelings of which I had no awareness. I relived buried scenes with pen and paper—the words taking me back as if I were there. My writing showed me the pain and hurt I felt around money, and that I'd been pretending when I thought money didn't matter to me.

I discovered that one benefit of writing my money memoir was that it taught me to listen and value my own thoughts and feelings, and to find my own truth. It enabled me to put pieces of my life together in new ways and to make new meaning of events. Writing the money memoir helped me to make sense of my money life in a way that nothing else had before.

Telling stories is especially vital to women, providing a means for us to know about ourselves, learn from one another, and pass on information. Much emotional benefit is gained through remembering, sharing, and giving and receiving support. For now I will just comment that, because we live in a male-dominated society, women's stories are often lost or ignored. And because we talk so little about money, our money stories have been largely lost to ourselves as well. We no longer recognize the value our stories hold.

Your stories are at the heart of *Emotional Currency*, and I strongly encourage you to write a money memoir. In case you are thinking it will be too hard to do, I guarantee that it won't be. Most people have found it easier, and of more value, than they anticipated. Even if you are resistant to writing, even if you hated writing in school, if you follow the guidance in this chapter, you should be able to push through your resistance. I assure you that you, too, will be surprised at how engaging this kind of writing can be. But if you still feel reluctant to even try writing, don't worry. Follow all the suggestions in this chapter but only in your thoughts, without writing them down.

To write your money memoir, I recommend you get a blank journal of some kind. The journal will be like a ledger, an accounting of your emotional relationship to money. There is no prescribed order or formula to follow. Include your experiences with money in the present as well as in the past. There's no need for the entries to be in chronological order. Keep your journal with you as you read through *Emotional Currency*, so you can jot down your thoughts and memories and answer the questions scattered throughout the book.

DISCOVERING YOUR TRUTH

A word about this kind of writing. There's no need for concern if you don't have a degree in creative writing or consider yourself a gifted writer. Not to worry if you haven't written a word beyond a grocery or to-do list since school. Memoir is part of women's long tradition of chronicling their lives through diaries, journal writing, and storytelling, and it has nothing to do with vocabulary or sentence structure.

This kind of writing has to do with discovering and connecting with your truth. This is writing for self-understanding and expression, not for publication. (Though I have to say, I've never heard or read a money story that wasn't captivating.) It doesn't have to be the big Truth—it just needs to be one of the ways of telling your story that rings true for you at this moment. And you are the only person who can say what you have to say.

No one will be critiquing what you write. We all learned in school to evaluate our writing, and we continue to grade ourselves. Being overly critical as you write will inhibit the flow of memory, so leave your inner critic behind. There is no such thing as a mistake—it's impossible to do this the wrong way. If you can get out of your own way and let the thoughts, feelings, and words flow, your writing will take you to unexpected places.

Please keep your focus on yourself and your experience of money. Follow wherever your inner thoughts and curiosities take you. You can include anything that comes to mind, no matter how tangential to money it might seem—exchanges, people, family dynamics, memories, longings, lessons, and so on. Daily life can provide rich material to inspire your writing. Your response to how much you paid for the caffe latte or the car can lead to unexpected feelings and associations to your past. Follow it all. When you write about others, remember that you want to think about them in terms of what they reveal or taught you about money.

SMALL INCIDENTS, BIG INSIGHTS

It turns out that the emotional side of money is difficult to see directly. We can glimpse understanding by reflecting on incidents in our lives—both large and small—that involve money. We can then piece together our glimpses into some larger patterns. Bring along your magnifying glass, for it's often the smallest incident or feeling that leads to big insights. Watch for signs, both obscure and obvious. These signs will not necessarily have dollar signs on them. They may come in strange forms, seemingly unrelated to money.

For example, I noticed how when the shampoo bottle or toothpaste tube was close to empty, I would begin to look forward to being able to throw it out. I became curious about why I could possibly anticipate an empty bottle or tube with such pleasure. Upon examination, I saw my fantasy that, if I bought a new kind of shampoo or even a replacement bottle of the product I was using, it might finally be the perfect product for which I was continually searching. Out of my awareness, I discovered I had bought hook, line, and sinker the idea that there was a perfect product out there for me, and all I had to do was find it. I saw how I have a different economy for hair products, preferring the more expensive ones, than for face creams, where I've always purchased the cheaper brands. My curly hair has always presented a "management" challenge in my life, to varying degrees of frustration. So it made sense to me that I would throw more money at it, believing that the more expensive hair products would be superior. This led me to realize I have numerous personal economies, meaning that the same amount of money carries a different economic value to me depending on what I'm using it to buy.

These thoughts were small glimpses that, even as I write about them now, seem kind of silly. But these are the very kinds of seemingly silly details that I encourage you to explore and write down as they may well lead to larger understandings, as well as connect you, to your idiosyncratic and personal relationship to money.

As you write, don't think too hard about finding the next idea or the right answer to a question. Let the first thought or answer from your gut, feelings, and heart lead the way. Follow the flow of thoughts and feelings. If you need to analyze and interpret, leave it for later. And don't discard any thoughts, for they may well be very much on target, even if they don't appear to be at first. Remember to include joyful things along with painful ones. Even if you think you already know about your relationship with money, understand there is still much to learn. As you discover and explore your money stories, allow yourself to be surprised!

MONEY MEMOIR STORIES

Here are two examples of money memoir stories. Though there are endless topics to write about, both of these happen to involve families. The first story, one that a participant wrote in an Emotional Currency Workshop, was written in a 30-minute writing exercise:

I am twelve years old, clothes shopping in a department store with my mom. I have picked out an outfit—sweater, pants, and sandals, all from the conspicuously displayed expensive racks, the ones placed right where you come off the escalator and designed to seduce you before you look around.

The sweater is particularly expensive and fashionable and not very pragmatic. It cannot be combined with other clothing I already own, and it is not well-suited to either warm or cold weather. It is just beautiful and I want it.

I don't remember the details of why or how I get this outfit, but I do and I treasure it. It is empowering and thrilling the way clothes you love can be. At the same time, something is very uncomfortable about the purchase. As far back as I can remember I have felt guilty, remorseful, undeserving, frivolous, impractical, and ashamed when money is spent on me, and I still don't know where these feelings come from.

If the outfit had been on sale, that would have been okay (less guilt). If it had been expensive but extremely practical, that would have been more palatable. But this was walking into a regular department store and picking the most stylish, expensive, put-together thing on display and buying it—and it was unstomachable for some reason. This was the only time anyone has done this for me, and I have never done this for myself as an adult.

My mother's parents were midwestern farmers who moved to Southern California and led working-class lives while running a quasi-suburban farm in a largely agricultural/suburban area. They grew their own food, canned and preserved, raised chickens and rabbits for food. They had bulk items like large quantities of cheese, which as an adult, I now know were government-subsidized food. My grandfather worked for the railroad, then Sears, and supported five children in a very frugal and self-sufficient lifestyle. My mother remembers sitting on the back of a moving pickup truck and shooting small animals, which the family would eat. They recycled everything. There was no luxury. My grandparents, who both lived into their nineties, never had trash service, no doubt because of cost and self-sufficiency. My grandfather, who died at the age of ninety-six—turns out he had over half a million dollars in various nest eggs—cash, savings, bonds, ancient and new stocks.

Where do my values end and my neurosis begin? I feel I was meant on some level, some very good and deep level, to be a farmer. I have always held on to this inner calling by doing what I could, be it letting my city apartment be overtaken by houseplants, or now coming as close as I can to a small urban farm with a large vegetable garden and chickens. I get such joy from this. It feels right. And yet, it is deeply entwined with a darker side, feeling undeserving of money or luxury. There is beauty in conservation, ecology, living simply, using few resources; small is better. These are deeply held beliefs of mine, and yet there is a cost and a dark side: messages I have gotten from somewhere that money is ignoble, that it corrupts—used as a justification for the pain of feeling either incapable or undeserving.

The second story is my own. It's one of the stories from my money memoir, one that takes a story to the next step of insight and reflection given that I've rewritten it several times. I've filled in some information so that it makes sense to you. It also illustrates how grabbing hold of a memory or feeling can take us on an illuminating journey.

The following passage was inspired by my experience at a checkout counter with a woman who had a red, wallet that was bulging with notes, receipts, coins, paper bills, and credit cards. It was encircled by several rubber bands holding everything in place, just like my mother used on her wallet. I hadn't thought of my mother's wallet in years, and my first thought became the first sentence of what I wrote in my money memoir:

My mother's wallet was always open to me. Inside, there was plenty of cash, usually some twenties and assorted other denominations. It was all there for my taking.

My father carried his bills in a money clip and, though it lay on top of the dresser whenever he was home, I have no memory of ever touching it. It was my mother who I would ask for cash. She would tell me to get her purse and help myself to what I needed. Invariably, she would call out, "Be sure you take enough."

Between whatever my mother had inherited from her parents and whatever my father earned from working hard in his business, we had plenty. Mom came from money, and she had always had more than she needed. Money was just there, even during the Depression, so she had never really concerned herself with it. Sharing it gave her great pleasure. She lovingly indulged me—I can now say overindulged, not just with cash but with whatever I wanted.

My father started to worry about money at the age of nine when his own father died and the pension the family received provided barely enough to get by. My grandmother never did have to go to work, but my father, even when quite young, worked after school and during the summer. He had planned to become a lawyer like his father, but because he graduated from college during the Depression, going on with his schooling was impossible, he felt lucky just to get a job. He was employed as an accountant, which reinforced his focus on money and made him adept, later in life, at managing our family's finances.

Some Sunday evenings on our way home from a day at the beach, my family would stop for five-cent ice cream cones at the Sav-On Drugstore. Across the street was Cost Plus, a store with lots of inexpensive merchandise from exotic places. The store was huge and filled with row after row of large bins, each with a heaping mound of some item. My father liked the practical things, while my mother and I were drawn to the more unusual.

One time I recall, I sorted through a bin of hand-carved wooden combs from India decorated with bright pink and purple strings, until I found just the right one. With longing in my heart and comb in hand, I approached my father and asked if he would buy it for me, for it was his approval I needed when I was with both my parents. I can still feel the humiliation as he shook his head and said, "What would you want that for?"

It never occurred to him that such a small thing could symbolize so much to me. He believed only in what was practical and this decorative comb had no utilitarian value whatsoever. This story, of asking and being denied, was repeated with a wide variety of requests I made to my father. His reactions continually reinforced that money is more important than anything else in the world and that one had better hold on to it tightly, not give it away, and not use it frivolously.

I tried to win my father's approval by earning good grades and school honors. He barely seemed to notice. I tried to engage him by playing tennis, but my ineptitude at the game only irritated him. When I asked for help with my homework, he had little patience and would end up finishing it himself. Again, the larger meaning—of wanting his time and attention—escaped him. I gave up trying to get his attention.

At this point in my money memoir, I stopped to think about what these memories taught me. After a while, I continued:

From my mother, I learned that things should come easily, including money, without having to work for them. From my father, I learned that I couldn't have what I wanted, including money, even if I tried. From both my parents' reactions to me, I came to believe that I wasn't deserving—from my mother because she gave her support so unconditionally that I never had to prove myself to her and from my father because I never could earn his support. It's taken me years to learn to work hard for what I want and not to give up when there are challenges.

YOUR FIRST MONEY MEMORY

I'm going to ask you to start your money journal with the question:

- What is my first memory of money from my childhood?

Take a moment to recall a scene, a conversation, an image. Once you have something in mind, put your pen to paper. It's fine, if you write just a few sentences or if you write pages. In time, you may recall even earlier memories, but this first memory is a significant one and a good beginning for your money memoir. Here's my first memory of money:

My first memory is of my brother, thirteen years older than I, holding me up so that I could reach the enormous whiskey bottle full of pennies on his chest of drawers. I was about two years old and I can still hear the clinking sound the coins made as they fell down the long neck of the bottle and hit the other pennies lying on the bottom.

HOW TO GET STARTED

Here are questions and suggestions for writing to help you start to write your money memoir. There are more questions at the end of this chapter as well as questions that appear throughout the book, for you to use as jumping-off points for your writing. For now, consider:

- What are a few of the exchanges you recall concerning money between you and your mother?
- Between you and your father?
- What is your first positive memory involving money?
- Your first negative memory involving money?
- What are your earliest memories of money coming into your possession—either given to you or your earning, saving, and even spending money?
- Describe your family's financial status when you were growing up.
- Did your family consider itself to be rich, poor, or in the middle?
- Was there always enough money?
- Did you have a piggy bank or a place you kept your money?
- Did anyone ever take or use your money?
- Did you ever take money that wasn't yours to take?
- How did you imagine things would be for you financially when you grew up?
- In what ways has your financial situation reflected or not reflected that vision?

Another approach you might try is to focus on relationships and write about people with whom you have had money dealings:

- Focus on a person, an object, or an incident and write everything that comes to mind, without concern about coherent sentences or flowing ideas. Then choose one or more of them to explore in more depth. Sometimes the list won't lead to anything you wish to write or think about further, but may well get your memories flowing, which has its own value. All memories and thoughts will help further ground you in your experience of money. For example, thinking about coins brought these thoughts to the surface for me: playing with the change in my father's little change tray on the silent butler where his jacket, which smelled of a mix of cigars and wool, hung; milk money in my lunch box; the tooth fairy leaving me quarters under my pillow; finding coins underneath the couch pillows; my shock at discovering that the only way to get the coins out of my piggy bank was to smash it.

- Focus on money through a particular period of time (for example, during your twenties, or when you left home), a particular person (such as your grandfather or first boss), a personal exchange (such as going clothes shopping with your mother or sharing expenses with your husband/partner), a family situation (such as asking your parents for a loan or needing to help support your mother), a defining moment (for example, when your partner or spouse admitted having a $20,000 debt, or learning you were eligible for a scholarship), or an event (such as your husband telling you he wants a divorce, or your mother telling you she lost much of her savings in the stock market). Describe what happened in relation to money in those situations and your feelings about it.

Use the everyday occurrences that spark your memories or curiosity about your relationship to money as starting points. These may include incidents and dramas as well as random questions, such as:.

- What made me choose to buy this particular table, necklace, jar of peanut butter, or pen?
- What makes me financially envious of the woman I work with, or someone who was at a meeting, or the person who lives next door?
- How do I feel about having someone clean my house? How do I feel about having more (or less) money than she does?

On the most basic level, writing your memoir will help you to see "what is so" about your relationship to money. Though it is enormously helpful to our exploration about money to talk with others, it is equally important, and in fact essential, for us to also explore our relationship to money on our own. Writing your memoir provides a structure for thinking and feeling about money without any input from others. In certain ways, we can see ourselves more clearly when we are privately looking, without having to anticipate or deal with the reactions and feelings of others. Without concern for presenting a certain image or protecting ourselves, we can let our guard down and feel and see things we might not be able to in the presence of others, even trusted friends. (And the opposite is true as well—that we are able to see things with others that we cannot see on our own.)

Another benefit of writing your money memoir is that as you gather snippets and stories, new understandings and patterns will begin to emerge. Much like rediscovering a long-lost photograph album of your past, your money memoir will provide scenes for you to observe. Contemplating the collected stories will help you make new connections within your past, as well as new connections between your past and your current behavior.

And lastly, writing a memoir is a healing process for many women. Remembering, retelling, and reliving past events can often be therapeutic. It could be a decision about our self-worth that was based on how an employer dealt with us in relationship to money that needs to be revisited. Or a traumatic story of money from the perspective of our childhood that needs the input of our adult perspective in order to heal. Or a story that needs our forgiveness, either toward ourselves or another. Each retelling offers the potential to reveal new aspects of the story and the possibility for making new connections.

Know that healing can happen at any point in the process of writing, reading, or pondering your money memoir. Healing wounds and confusions from your past will help you relate to money more fully in your present life. It can be helpful to have pen and paper close at hand to jot the thoughts and images as they occur to you. I find some of my most compelling new insights fly away quickly, even though in the moment they feel solidly anchored in my memory.

The following questions are meant to stimulate your memory and help you create your money memoir. There is no need to consider them all at one time; you can refer back to them as you move through the book. In addition, each successive chapter concludes with a list of pertinent questions.

- How old were you when you first realized what money was?
- What one pivotal event dealing with money do you recall and in what ways did it affect you?
- Was anyone else involved?
- If so, in what role(s)?
- How did your mother view money?
- How did your father view money?
- How did your parents each feel about the money they had?
- In what ways did it matter to your parents to have, or not have, more money?
- Were there people outside the family who influenced you regarding money?
- If so, in what ways?
- What decisions did you make about money when you were younger?
- Did you ever feel guilty about receiving something you didn't feel you deserved?
- How important has it been for you to have money? In what ways has it been important?
- How often do you think about money?
- Under what conditions?

CURRENT MONEY DILEMMA

Draw a line down the middle of a piece of paper. On the left side of the page, write a money situation you face. On the right side, write your feelings about money in that situation. For instance, "Buying a new car" goes on the left hand side. On the right hand side go the feelings that you have about money and the decision to buy a new car. Include what you think and feel right now as well as any past thoughts or feelings that might inform your decision. Don't worry if the statements contradict themselves—they will! So what you write might include all of these thoughts: "I don't want to have a car payment," "I'm afraid my older car might break down," "I'm attached to my old car," "I believe it's best to drive a car until it falls apart," "I'm embarrassed driving my beat-up car," "I like to have an older car rather than a newer one," "I want the new bells and whistles of a later model car," and "I have difficulty deciding what to buy to replace my old car." Reflect on what you have written and make any connections with your past that might occur to you. Your decision is more likely to be a good one for you when you've considered all your conflicting thoughts and feelings.

You are the only one capable of finding the

right place for money in your life.

CHAPTER 3

What Shapes Your Relationship to Money?

Whenever I want to buy myself something special, I argue with myself before the
purchase, as well as afterward, spoiling any pleasure I might have gotten. —AMY

A STAGGERING MIX OF INDIVIDUAL, social, and cultural influences comes together to shape us as people and to shape our relationship to money. Although we share commonalities and behavior patterns from our culture and human wiring, we are all very different. Of the more than seven billion humans alive, how astounding it is that no two of us are exactly the same!

A multitude of influences shapes our money lives—so many, in fact, that it would be impossible to explore them all in this or any book. However, over the years I've seen certain recurring influences in the lives of my clients and Emotional Currency Workshop participants, and those are the influences that I will focus on in this chapter: psychological issues, taboos concerning speaking about money, familial expectations and limitations, materialism, financial resources, immigration, and race. Each of these influences provides a perspective from which to observe your relationship to money.

ISSUES THAT SHAPE YOUR RELATIONSHIP TO MONEY

Our individual psychological makeup shapes how we deal with ourselves and others, and how we deal with money. And like a chameleon, money serves whatever psychological need we have for it. We may, for example, try to bolster our self-worth by earning—or saving—a lot of money, while others might use the opposite behavior of spending all they can, out of the same desire to increase their self-worth. We may spend every penny we earn in an attempt to fulfill our desire for abundance—and to fight off feelings of deprivation. Whereas another person will hoard money to arrive at the same feelings of abundance. So behavior alone does not indicate exactly what the underlying motivation is.

In the next section, we'll briefly explore five psychological issues that intertwine with money: self-worth, abundance and deprivation, protection, autonomy and dependency, and envy. As we do, reflect on how these—and other psychological issues—may impact your own relation to and use of money.

Self-worth

In the United States, money is viewed as *the* measure of success and failure. With our cultural emphasis on individualism and competition, it's difficult not to judge ourselves and others, at least to some degree, by financial status. And, in fact, some people base their sense of identity and merit on money alone.

Wealth is seen as a reward for ability and effort, and wealthy people often see themselves, and are seen by many others, as superior to people who are not rich. Poverty is thought to be a personal failure. We fear poverty and the poor. And we know that poor people, ourselves included if we should join their ranks, are thought to have little value as human beings. Often we value the wealthy investment banker more than the poor convenience store clerk without knowing anything about who they are or how they live. And yet, is the woman waiting to take the bus after work necessarily less important to the world than the woman parked next to the bus stop in her new Mercedes? Or is the artist really of little value until her artwork is commercially successful? And some of us, at least some of the time, flip the measurement of value on its end, valuing the convenience store clerk just because she is poor and devaluing the investment banker because she is wealthy.

Having, spending, and earning money make many of us feel valuable on a superficial level. Even though we know that money can't really define our authentic sense of self-worth, we may still feel our self-worth grow as our income rises or when we have a big wad of money in our wallet or a large account balance. Money can shore us up from feelings of emptiness, worthlessness, and self-doubt. And certainly, we use money at times to soothe, calm, and reassure ourselves, just as we might have used a special toy or blanket when we were young. We can use it as a distraction from self-critical feelings. And we fantasize that money can keep all sorts of inner demons and wolves at bay.

But money can't buy a solid, well-developed sense of self or of self-worth. And a life that revolves around *only* money cannot bring a rich interior or external life. Handled well, money relieves us of preoccupation with anxiety about our survival, and it provides opportunities and experiences that help us develop healthy self-worth, a self-worth that comes from how we *are* in the world instead of from what we have.

From the time Kris was able to formulate such a thought, she connected her low self-esteem to growing up poor. When she entered the workforce she set herself the goal of making X number of dollars, a secret figure that only she knew, with the idea that X dollars would bring self-esteem. But when her net worth reached X amount of dollars, much to her disbelief, her self-worth barely budged. Though making money over the years had elevated her self-esteem, the deeper layers of inadequacy required a shift in her relationship to herself that money could not bring.

Questions that ask how money influences your self-esteem and sense of your self:

- What are some of the connections you experience between money and self-worth?
- In what ways, and under what circumstances, do you judge yourself for what you have?
- And how do you judge others for what they appear to have?

- How do you feel when you are with someone who is poorer than you?
- How do you feel when you are with someone who is wealthier than you?
- Do you see yourself differently when those around you have more or less than you have?
- In terms of contributing to your sense of self, where would you rank money?
- Do you imagine that if your net worth reaches a certain level you will feel better about yourself?
- If so, in what ways?
- And how did you determine this figure?

Abundance and Deprivation

Our feelings of abundance and deprivation can come directly from the financial conditions we grew up with, the atmosphere at home when we were growing up, or our current financial state. However, feelings of abundance or deprivation don't necessarily coincide with our financial wealth or poverty. Some people who grow up "with nothing" report feeling they always "had enough." While others who never knew want, feel consistently deprived. These patterns can continue into adulthood.

We often use money to symbolize our feelings of abundance and deprivation, meaning that money is a mirror that does not reflect how much money we actually have, but rather it reflects our inner psychological state. We all experience feelings of both abundance and deprivation, and one or the other may tend to be dominant at different times in our lives. And though they can be seen as opposites, I prefer to see them on a continuum.

Abundance is the feeling of plenty, of having enough. It can be a momentary sensation, perhaps from an unexpectedly high balance in our checking account or purchasing a special purse we've wanted. But in the fullest experience of abundance, it's a sense that there will be enough today, enough tomorrow, and enough in the foreseeable future. Feeling or embracing abundance is an ability to enjoy what money we have with ownership and gratitude. It doesn't necessarily involve extravagance; it may well be a thoughtful or careful use of money. But there is always a sense of freedom and expansiveness that comes from the experience of abundance, a sense of well-being about our ability to provide for ourselves or be taken care of by others. Generosity and a desire to share seem to naturally flow from it.

Deprivation is the feeling of scarcity, of not having enough. It is the absence of something that was there, or that we think should have been there; it involves something being taken away, withheld, or lost. It is a sense of being at a disadvantage. Poverty is the deprivation of the basic necessities for survival, the things that most of us take for granted. A lack or shortage of funds, a sudden loss of money, or a gift withheld can evoke feelings of deprivation within us.

The question "Are you someone who sees the glass as half empty or half full?" reflects our feelings about abundance and deprivation. What we see—a glass half empty or a glass half full—is largely determined by our inner state. While this inner state may be influenced by how much money we had growing up, came to have, or currently have, it's also based on all sorts of other deprivations and abundances in our lives, involving qualities, experiences, relationships, or things. Did we feel loved? Did we have a capacity for friendships? Did we receive attention and feel that we mattered? Did we feel accomplished and smart in some way? Did we do things that were inspiring and engaging to us? Did others find us in someway appealing? We don't get to have everything in life, but how much we have of what matters to us contributes to how empty or full we feel.

We learn to use money to compensate for deprivations in our life, to use it as a salve for that which we have never had, or no longer have. For some, making, saving, or hoarding money is a way to balance out the feelings of not having enough in other arenas in their lives. Giving to ourselves—by buying things, services, and experiences—can be an attempt to compensate for or fill up the places of loss in our lives.

An extreme illustration of a compensatory use of money is the story of Sally, a woman I interviewed, whose parents owned six houses around the world and who were constantly flitting from one to another of them to attend parties and glamorous events. Sally spent the school year at their home in Virginia, staying primarily with the staff of the house. Her parents would come to spend several weeks or a month with her before they departed to their other lives. The way Sally would learn that they had left was by finding an envelope, with her name written on the front and a check inside, left on foyer table in the entry way. Sometimes there would be a short note telling her to be a good girl while they were away, sometimes not. The check was a stand in for her parents. It was their attempt to make up for, to compensate for, neglecting her.

In many ways Sally had abundance in her life. But she experienced deprivation in terms of what she needed most—the love and attention and presence of her parents. She experienced massive emotional deprivation in the midst of material abundance. Sally could have responded in many ways to these conditions. Luckily, there had been a positive mother figure for her in the woman who was paid to take care of her. (As is not uncommon in very wealthy families, some of the adults she formed the closest attachments to were among her parents' staff.) As an adult, she did the inner work necessary that enabled her to value what her surrogate mother had given her, healing the wounds from her real mother and finding an emotional abundance within herself. And she established her own relationship to money, which involved living simply and being philanthropic.

The power of our inner states is also evident in the lives of people with wealth who, even with multiple millions of dollars, feel that they don't have enough money to buy things for themselves—things that many of us don't find at all extravagant, say going out to eat or buying a new pair of shoes. They feel deprived, and they use money to reinforce their sense of deprivation by continually denying themselves, even in the face of having so much. And of course the contrasting pattern is also true, where we ignore our limited resources and use money—to buy things, take vacations, give gifts, and make donations—which cultivates a feeling of abundance. Out of these feelings of abundance, we act as if we have more money than we do—something that's so easy to do with credit cards.

For decades, abundance dominated the collective consciousness of the United States. Although there have always been many who fell outside of it, as a society we only acknowledged the upwardly mobile standard of living. It has taken our country's struggling financially for us to rediscover the value of going without. Some have painfully fallen into poverty and the uncertainty of unemployment, but for others a belt tightening has been adequate. Collectively we are beginning to tolerate a sense of deprivation and frugality. We are healthier individually and societally if we can tolerate both feelings of deprivation and abundance as both states are a part of the natural cycle of life and a part of the natural cycle of emotional life. To feel them is to experience the unavoidable fact that life both gives and takes away.

Questions on abundance and deprivation:

- How do feelings of abundance and deprivation play out in your relationship to money?
- Do you tend to see the glass half empty or half full in general?
- Do you feel the same with regard to money?
- What gives you a sense of abundance (with money)?
- What gives you a sense of deprivation (with money)?

Protection

Money protects us from some of the harshness of life. With enough money, we no longer constantly deal with survival needs or having unanticipated expenses turn our lives upside down; we have more control over our environment and can put our emotional energy to use in other ways. Having money also shelters us from certain kinds of dangers by allowing us to live in safer neighborhoods, feed ourselves and our families, have reliable transportation, have access to medical care, and sometimes even plan our future. Money insulates us from the feelings of despair, insecurity, anxiety, fear, and anger that can accompany poverty.

In addition to the many concrete ways that money can protect us, we also imagine unrealistic ways in which we think it can protect us. We fantasize that money can protect us from all sorts of human suffering, from the risks and pain of living. We fantasize that money buys control over our lives and over others, and perhaps even secretly imagine that the rich don't really have problems. (Of course, there's a grain of truth in this because you can buy yourself out of some kinds of problems— wealthy white collar criminals receive much more lenient sentences than poor people who have committed far less serious crimes. People who can afford it have insurance to soften the blow of all sorts of losses, including property, the capacity to work, and life.) But having money doesn't protect the wealthy or their family members from car accidents, diseases, marital problems, substance abuse, physical abuse, psychiatric problems, sexual addictions, and all the other problems and issues everyone faces. The wealthy even have money problems, ones that sometimes tear families apart.

When I was working on my doctorate in psychology and I mentioned to someone that I was doing research on women with inherited wealth, invariably that person would comment, "How can they have any problems?" or "Wish I had their problems." I think most of us deeply believe that money makes life substantially better. (And of course, it can. Especially if one is poor, getting more money can bring great relief as basic needs are met.) But even the rich have problems. Peggy, a woman I interviewed for my research, told me that her mother simply could not understand how Peggy could be depressed given the sizeable inheritance she had received from her grandmother. The mother, a woman who had grown up with wealth herself, told her daughter, "Just go to Europe and get over it." Though Peggy knew Europe wasn't the cure, she also felt ashamed that it wasn't—for she, too, had internalized the belief that because of her inheritance she should now be carefree.

Too much money—depending how we choose to live with it, relate to it, and use it—can actually provide too much protection from ordinary life, which creates other kinds of problems in our psyches. It can act like a cocoon that insulates us from life. It can make us unable to take care of ourselves and dependent on others for our maintenance. All the necessary tasks of life—be they earning money, shopping for groceries and preparing meals, picking up the kids from school, planning our schedules, or paying the bills—help us to develop life skills and provide important grounding in our lives. These daily activities give us direction, meaning, a sense of accomplishment, and connect us to the rhythms of our life. Without them, our capacity for psychological growth can be severely limited.

Questions about safety and vulnerability:

- In what ways does money represent protection to you?

- When have you experienced being protected by money?
- And in what ways?
- When have you experienced being unprotected by money?
- And in what ways?
- Have you ever felt overly protected because of money or wealth?
- Have you ever felt vulnerable or unsafe from either not having or having money?

Autonomy and Dependency

Money is an extremely good avenue by which we can express our needs for autonomy and dependency. We all need to be both autonomous and dependent—that is, we need to both be able to rely on ourselves to provide what we need as well as be able to rely on others to provide for us. Depending on our life experiences and our emotional deficits and assets, we may not trust that we can provide for ourselves and so become overreliant on others. Or we may distrust the ability of others to help us and so decide to rely only on ourselves. Or our parents may have needed us to remain dependent upon them financially and discouraged us from taking care of ourselves and being independent. Sometimes we insisted that, through word and deed, they bail us out. And some of us may decide that we had best be completely independent either because of our parents' incapacity to help us or because of the price we had to pay for their assistance was too high.

One such example is Sonja, whose reaction to her childhood poverty was to vow that she would never again be in such a powerless and dependent state. She said, "Based on the utter failure of my parents to give us a stable home, I decided the only way I could be safe was to make good money myself. Working hard became my whole life, and I made more money than I thought was possible. For years, I loved being so strong and independent, it made me very happy—until it didn't. In my midthirties, I became increasingly lonely and realized that my not needing anyone was no longer a good solution for me."

Sonja knew she had to face the emotional walls that blocked her from sharing her life with another. She went on to say, "In the Emotional Currency Workshop, I came to see how I was trying to avoid being vulnerable, not just financially but emotionally, too. I was using money to hide behind. So I started to chip away at my habits with money, first at the edges. I decided to spend money on myself and give some money away, things I couldn't ever do when all my efforts were going toward having enough money to ensure I never needed anyone else. I also asked friends to help me when I moved, instead of hiring someone to do it. And on several occasions when friends reached for the restaurant check, I let them pick it up rather than always insisting that I pay my own way."

None of these were easy things for Sonja to do, but she did them, because her longings for connection became stronger than her difficulty in relying on others. And slowly, it actually began to feel good to her to depend on others emotionally, and she could make new choices in her life.

At the other end of the continuum are those who are unable to provide for themselves, those who are either in need of partial assistance or full support. Often they look to a spouse or a parent to help them. Some even have good incomes, but their money behaviors lead them to not be able to live within their means, and they are always in need of financial help.

We often have an unconscious wish to be taken care of, either because we feel that we are inadequate, not able to provide for ourselves, or are afraid of taking on the challenges in the world required to support ourselves. We may have never been taken care of well before and still long to be taken care of. These unconscious wishes, unless dealt with, get played out with our loved ones and families.

Sometimes we find ourselves in dependent financial situations that necessitate our suppressing parts of ourselves. Romantic partnerships often require that we repress or bury aspects of ourselves for the greater good of the union, but this can be intensified when there is also financial dependency. And all the more so when we stay in a partnership primarily for that reason.

A client told me that she had deeply loved her husband and felt they shared an egalitarian relationship in most ways. But because her husband had earned much more money than she had, she yielded to his opinions about important decisions in their marriage. When he died, she realized that submitting to his desires had necessitated her to submerge competent and opinionated aspects of herself. These aspects had come alive after his death, and were proving invaluable in her continuing on without him. She regretted that she had abandoned her point of view so often in the marriage.

Questions concerning autonomy and dependency:

- In what ways have you been financially dependent?
- In what ways have you been financially autonomous?
- Are you/would you like to be taken care of financially, either completely or partially?
- If so, by whom?
- Or do you prefer to earn your own way?
- How has it felt to be taken care of financially?
- Either as a child and/or an adult?
- Were there strings attached to the money?
- If you are currently being taken care of financially, how is it for you?
- And are there strings attached?
- If you are self-supporting, at what age did you start to support yourself?
- How was that for you?
- Do you fantasize about being taken care of?
- Or being self-supporting?
- What does that fantasy look like?

Envy

We all feel envy. It may be a fleeting flash of feeling or something that lingers and shows up frequently in our lives. We envy the good qualities, the good money, or the good life that others have. We want to live as they do, but because of an inner sense of emptiness, we don't think that we can ever achieve what they have. And out of our pain of their having and our not having, we objectify the people we envy and are only able to see them as the part of their lives that we envy. We turn them into a thing. Part of this process is not unlike gender stereotyping, in which women are objectified—seen only as objects, not complex and real people—and thought to be incompetent or weak just because they are female. So with money we stereotype the people we envy as, for example, rich and powerful. And out of our envy we either idealize them for being rich and powerful, or we deflate them for being rich and powerful. Envy can take the form of exalted praise or denigrating criticism.

Envy is unpleasant, for both the envier and the envied. Being envied is painful enough that some of us avoid it by not acquiring, achieving, or accomplishing things that others might envy. This is more often the case for women, who frequently are uncomfortable being the object of envy. Heirs who choose to give away their fortunes are motivated by many factors, of which deflecting envy can be one. It's also one of the reasons that people with wealth sometimes are careful not to show that they have money.

Julia, a client, talked about her friend, Helen, who buys anything she likes and constantly takes expensive vacations. Julia knows that Helen has suffered much sorrow and guilt over a schizophrenic brother who was institutionalized at the age of twenty-two. But when gripped by envy, Julia can only see Helen's large financial resources. And she resents her friend for having so much while she, Julia, has so little in comparison.

Kendra started working two jobs to support her family after her husband lost his job. Her sister-in-law, Alison, who does not work, often complains to Kendra about how much she has to take care of. Alison doesn't seem to appreciate the difference between the tasks she is doing—keeping up her two homes or getting ready for the next family vacation—and what Kendra is doing—carrying her family's entire financial burden. Kendra doesn't want to be Alison, but she is envious of the lack of financial burden in her sister-in-law's life that allows her to be so oblivious. And she secretly wants something to happen to Alison so that she has to suffer, too.

Like Kendra, out of our envy we may wish to destroy the good the other person has. This occurs generally within our psyches, though some people act out their envy through stealing or undermining the good that another has. Envy often takes place in work settings and in families. It is part of what drives family wars over wills—the kind of battles in which a large amount of the inheritance is spent on litigation. It's, "If I can't have it, then I don't want her to have it, and I'll do whatever I can to destroy it."

We can tell we are being envied when we are treated in an inappropriately idealized or deflated fashion. The envier is not interested in knowing us as we are or in any kind of wholeness, but rather only in an objectified way, such as the struggling artist, financial wizard, trust-fund baby, successful entrepreneur, or wealthy aristocrat. In these stereotypical ways—along with all the other possible stereotypes surrounding money—we are judged as either perfect and idealized, or as impaired and demonized.

Ann and Barry Ulanov, in their book *Cinderella and Her Sisters: The Envied and the Envying*, state, "The false issue, so tempting to both envier and envied, is to ask, why does one of us have the good and the other not? There can only be one answer: it must be your fault or my fault. Both possibilities are caught in our attempts to control the good and its distribution. Of course, the true issue lies elsewhere, in the problem of how to discover and relate to the good, where to find it, how to nourish it."

This was the way out of envy for Julia and Kendra, to feel their envy and then find and amplify the good in their own lives. As with envy's sibling emotion, shame, if we can allow ourselves to feel it, either the envy or the experience of being envied, and consciously explore it, we become more human.

Questions about envy:

- What kinds of envy do you feel, or have you felt, regarding money?
- Who have you been envious of financially?
- What were you envious of?
- Were you ever envious of something your sibling had?
- Are you envious now?
- Have you ever been envied because of money?

Greed

And lastly, just the briefest mention of greed, the desire for more wealth or possessions than we need. It comes from wanting what we don't have and wanting to protect what we do have. Most of us have this deadly sin as well. We may not have the Wall Street version, but we live in a greedy world, and it's contagious. If you look for it, you'll find greed somewhere in your money interactions. A financial planner with very wealthy clients once told me, "Everyone wants more money than they have." She stated this with such absolute assuredness that I could only guess that what she said was true in her world. I think she was talking about greed, without knowing it. However, I know people, extremely wealthy and not, who feel no need or desire for more money.

Questions about greed:

- Do you know financially greedy people?
- Are any of them from your family?
- Are there circumstances in which you feel greedy about money?
- Or about having things? (Describe in detail.)

THE TABOO AGAINST
TALKING ABOUT MONEY

Culture determines how we talk about money or whether, in fact, we talk about it at all. We are so used to the cultural taboo regarding talking about money that we are hardly aware of it. And yet that taboo undermines women's relationship to money.

With the taboo in place, there's not much to say to one another about money. Our financial conversations tend to be about where to find good deals and the high price of groceries, child care, housing, vacations, credit card interest, and gas. Perhaps we talk about being broke or money being tight. We don't share the dollar figure of our debts or assets. And if we do talk, we heavily censor what we share. A Chinese American friend visiting China was surprised when her Chinese dining partner asked the waitress, a complete stranger, how much money she made. The waitress very matter-of-factly reported the sum. In the United States, most of us don't even have a clue of what our best friends' salaries are.

And in our families, conversations about money rarely take place. Anxiety and stress may be thick in the air, but given the taboo against talking about money, actually talking about the money situation at hand might never happen. We want to know if our aging parents have enough savings to take care of themselves should one of them require more care, but when we mention the word money our dads change the topic.

In Elisabeth's case, a simple conversation with her father, which never took place, would have been enormously clarifying. She described, "I started to receive an annual gift from a trust my grandfather left me when I was twenty four. It went directly into an investment account that my father invested. I was living poorly on my salary in Manhattan, and that annual gift would have definitely made my life a lot less difficult. The irony is that years later I discovered my father would have been fine giving me the money to use, but I had no idea at the time. It was so taboo to talk about money that my father never explained the trust to me and I couldn't ask him about it. Money was never spoken about in my family, even though my father was a banker. The only thing I ever heard him say about our finances was, 'We're comfortable.'"

However, when we are given permission and encouragement to share our personal experience of money, we have lots to say to one another. An exercise near the beginning of an Emotional Currency Workshop illustrates how hungry we all are to talk about money. I give participants two blank index cards: on the first, I ask them to write something in their money lives that is causing them difficulty that they would be able to share with a few other women. On the second, I ask them to write something that they are struggling with around money that they would not want to share with anyone else because it causes them too much shame or pain to talk about. When they are done, I tell them to put the second card away securely in their notebooks or purses, that there is no need for them to share what it says with anyone. With permission to keep their money-secret to themselves, the participants feel freer to breach the cultural taboo and begin sharing with one another. Although they are never asked to, often by the end of the workshop, several women have shared what felt too hard to talk about when they began.

Ask yourself what you would write on your cards:

- What is something in your money life that is causing you difficulty—something concrete that you can explore and talk about?
- What is another difficulty with money that you feel too ashamed or embarrassed to share with others?

I tell women in my groups that talking about money will inevitably cause each of them to feel shame, either before they speak, while they are speaking, or after they have spoken. Breaking the taboo against talking about money evokes shame. I encourage them to share their stories, despite their feelings of shame. I promise that, if they can tolerate the embarrassment, humiliation, or shame, good things will come from it emotionally. I make the same promise to you as you read this book. Even if you only share your stories with yourself—it may be the first time you are aware of many of your feelings about money, and some of them may be uncomfortable—opening yourself up to them will bring positive results in the end.

In the groups, the women then go into pairs and take turns talking about what they wrote on their first card. The energy in the room electrifies as they share what for many are long-held secrets and hidden places. Whatever shame is there is only fleeting. The relief of sharing is palpable, as is the gratitude. Being listened to with respect and caring provides the support needed to explore this long-forbidden subject. This is what is denied us when we comply with the taboo against talking about money.

Other questions about this taboo:

- Were money matters discussed in your family?
- If so, in what manner were they discussed?
- Did your parents retreat to discuss money in private, or did such discussions take place openly?
- Who do you talk with about money?
- Who don't you talk with, but need to?
- Who don't you talk with, but want to?

- What comes up for you when you think about talking with friends and family about money?

FAMILY INFLUENCES

Our family of origin is a significant teacher about money. Families can use money in numerous ways: to express love, to manipulate, to support, to reward, to punish, to show favoritism, to control, to foster dependency, and more. In our families, we observe the ways money is intertwined with survival, status, work choices, and self-worth. Questions regarding family:

- In your family, did you learn that your basic needs for food, clothing, shelter, and love would be taken care of, at least enough of the time, to safely come to expect it?
- Did you learn it was okay to want what you wanted, or were you told—whether verbally or nonverbally—that what you wanted didn't matter?
- Was it okay to ask for more than you were given?
- Did you learn that it was safe to share, or did you sense you had better watch out for yourself?
- Did you learn that you had to take care of others at the expense of taking care of yourself?
- Did you learn that what belonged to you was yours, or were others allowed to take it without your permission?

When we look at our families, it is abundantly clear that money has everything to do with relationship. By seeing the ways in which money is handled in our families, we learn about give and take, sharing and withholding, power and powerlessness, belonging and exclusion, fear and comfort, and trust and distrust. Feelings of envy and competition often occur over what has been given, to whom it has been given, and what has been withheld. It is impossible for everyone to be treated exactly equally, and yet some parents and grandparents only exacerbate that pain by not even trying to hide their favoritism. We each respond in our own unique way to similar life lessons about money, and even in the same family, siblings can have very different responses. Also, over time, a family's financial circumstances can change radically, so siblings may experience quite different resources within the same family.

Sometimes we realize there were contradictions between what was said and what was done. How our parents felt about their financial status is often more influential than what their actual economic status was. For those who grew up with little, if their parent or parents weren't bothered by their hardship, they will feel differently about money than if they had grown up with a parent who was in continual pain or anxiety over marginal finances.

Your family has its own stories about money. It has its own idiosyncratic ideals and worries. It's a complicated tale of many generations, with lots of characters and twists and turns. Your parents add their own histories, feelings, attitudes, and beliefs about money to the mix. As their child, you have to bring together their disparate relationships to money and create your own. This task is easier if they themselves were able to join their two sensibilities about money to form a workable approach to money matters in your family. However, as in many cases, if they were not able to align their money lives or they divorced, the task of reconciling their two different money worlds fell more to you.

Amy could easily buy things for her children and her partner, but buying anything more than the basics for herself unleashed harsh self-criticism. Tired of standing in a store fighting with herself over whether to buy a pair of jeans, she decided she wanted to figure out why she had this inner battle.

When she came to an Emotional Currency Workshop, she described her dilemma this way:

I've tried to tell myself I deserve a new pair of jeans, that I wouldn't think twice about buying them for my kids. But unless mine are in shreds, a new pair for myself feels like I'm being too extravagant. Oh, I can get shampoo, get my haircut or my car fixed—the basics—just fine. But if I buy something just because I like it, clothes or something for the house, I'm in trouble—with myself. If I do manage to buy the jeans, my internal dialogue is so familiar, "Who do you think you are to want so much?" or "These don't fit exactly right, you shouldn't have bought them," and, of course, "They were too expensive." I'm far from frivolous with money, so it's not about the money. I'm just beating myself up.

Amy knew exactly where her internal struggle came from—her parents fought a lot about how money was spent in the family. But she needed to look at how she felt about her parents' fights before she could locate her own comfort with spending and having. She emotionally recounted being pulled into their fights:

My mother squirreled away money from her household budget to buy me whatever I wanted. I would hide the new dress or pair of shoes in my closet, wearing them secretly until they no longer looked brand new and they could pass underneath my dad's money radar. If my dad did discover something was new, there would be a terrible fight. My dad would yell, "We're all going to be in the poorhouse soon because your mother throws away money." My mother would try to explain that she always stayed within her household budget, but he was just angry. She'd end up sobbing in the bathroom behind a locked door.

Long after Amy's parents had died, the fallout from these arguments continued in her own mind. She realized she needed to learn more about why they had behaved the way they did. She recalled that her mother had grown up in a family where children never got what they wanted, creating a sense of real deprivation. Amy realized that her mother couldn't bear to let her go without something she wanted. "I could handle it," Amy explained. "But denying me something must have stirred up all her old longings and disappointments. She couldn't *not* buy things for me. My dad must have wounded that same place in her when he'd yell at her to stop spending money. That's why she'd flee into the bathroom, crying for that little girl in her who was punished for wanting something."

Appreciating the back story to the family fights helped release Amy from their continual repetition in her own life. Her internal conversation while shopping changed from having to prove to her father that she was worthy to trusting herself to know what she wanted and needed to buy.

We all struggle with our appetites, and our parents' beliefs and behaviors about what's okay to have and to want become entangled with our own. Sorting them out can be amazingly freeing. Like Amy, I was caught between my parents in their fights about money. My own money story begins in childhood:

When I was in grammar school, my half sister—whom I adored and who was sixteen years older than I and living on the other side of the country—seemed always urgently in need of a financial fix: loans to buy groceries or to turn the heat back on in winter. After my parents learned my sister was addicted to heroin, her pleas broadened to include cash to pay the drug dealer. My parents fought bitterly over whether to provide the money. My mother was willing to use all of her sizable inheritance to save my sister. My father literally became ill from the sums being spent. To me, it looked as though my "good" mother wanted to protect my sister while my "bad" father wanted to cut her off. (It didn't matter that he was the stepfather; he probably would have treated me in exactly the same fashion if I had been shooting his money up my arm.) From my young vantage point, it seemed that money was the only way to save my sister's life.

Once I began to uncover my own money stories, I came to appreciate the complexities of this family drama. My father had a deep-seated fear of being poor. His own father, a lawyer, had died when my dad was only nine, and the family was uprooted geographically and socioeconomically. They went from living in a large home with a comfortable and steady income to living in cramped apartments on a fluctuating pension, which didn't always provide enough money to get from month to month. Though my grandmother never went to work, my father augmented their income when he was young, first delivering newspapers, then caddying at a golf course, and eventually parking cars. He had the eldest child's sense of responsibility and watched out for my grandmother financially for as long as she was alive.

My mother, on the other hand, never worried about money, at least not until my sister's problems. Her own mother had come from a wealthy family and her father was a good businessman in his own right. Her first husband had made an excellent salary, which they spent on a fancy lifestyle that included upsacle homes and boarding school for their children. By the time she had divorced, met and married my father, and had me, my mother had a much simpler lifestyle. When my sister's addiction surfaced, my mother blamed herself. Out of her feelings of having failed as a mother and out of her love for her daughter, she gave my sister whatever she asked for. Having been prized for her beauty throughout her life, my mother didn't trust her own intelligence, and had learned, as wealthy people often do, to rely on a series of expensive experts for advice and guidance, in this case, to "fix" her daughter.

My insights into my parents' backgrounds made their battles more understandable. It became clear to me that money was the basis of security for both my mother and my father, only in opposite ways: saving money brought my father a sense of security in the face of a deep-seated fear of falling into poverty again, while spending money to overcome her own imagined deficiencies was my mother's route to feeling secure. Each of their coping strategies made the other feel more anxious and hopeless.

I had always believed they had divorced over money, but I came to realize that it was actually their inability to find ways to take care of each other through the family crisis that caused it. Rather than simply feeling angry at their limitations, in understanding them I uncovered my own compassion for the pain their emotional impairments brought each of them—and myself. That compassion allowed me to be close to my father again in the last years of his life and to understand why my mother had risked both her marriage and her financial future by continually giving my sister large sums of money.

I had learned from my family that money was about life and death. My sister's continual money emergencies deeply embedded within me the notion that having money prevented disaster. I circled around my family dramas for years, putting the pieces of the puzzle together and feeling the layers of grief, anger, and heartache. It came as quite a shock to me when I finally realized that it wasn't money that could have saved my sister. My mother and I had put all our hope in the wrong place: money. If there had been any chance of a solution to my sister's struggles, it would have had to come from a place deep inside of her. Once I realized that, money lost its lifesaving aura for me.

Questions concerning your family's role in your money story:

- What were the spoken money messages in your family?
- What were the unspoken messages?
- How did your parents treat you with regard to money and how did that feel?
- Was money used as a reward?
- As a punishment or in manipulative ways?
- Who handled money matters and in what way?
- How did your parents relate to one another around money?
- If they fought, what did they fight over?
- If your parents had problems dealing with money, what were they?
- Did you get an allowance?
- If so, what did you do with it?
- How did it compare to your siblings' or your friends' allowances?
- Did it ever get taken away as a punishment?
- If you earned money, did you get to keep it for yourself?
- What did you spend it on?
- Were comments made about how much things cost?
- About things your parents couldn't afford?
- About how much money other people had or spent?
- Was anyone in the family given more money than others were?
- Did you feel jealous of displays of love between other family members that involved money?
- Did your parents try to give an impression about their financial standing to the outside world that was different from their actual financial status?
- Did they use money in ways that were different from how they taught you to use it or think about it?
- Have there been dramas in your family that have involved money?
- How have they affected and influenced you?
- Did you then, or do you now, recognize any family patterns of money behavior?

- What stories involving money have been told in your family—and what stories have not been told?
- What was the family emotional legacy about money?
- In what ways are you now like your parents in terms of your relationship to money (spending, saving, worrying, earning, and so on)?
- In what ways are you not like your parents?

CULTURE

Cultural context plays an enormous role in how money functions and what it represents. Our culture—meaning the customs and social institutions we live under and the rules we live by—establishes a value for money, both literally and symbolically. It defines the role of money in our lives as well as which behaviors are considered ethical or unethical in relationship to money.

Money Rules

Money dominates our culture in the United States. Making money is the chief motivation of most activity in our society, which values material goods and accumulated wealth above all else. Money is treated as if it were an omnipotent god. We generally give power and preference to wealth over ability.

Almost everything in American culture is influenced by money. It touches where we live, what car we drive, what we eat, where our children go to school, whom we know, whether we have access to health care, whether we take vacations, and so many other choices and opportunities. It influences all the arts: what books get published, what art gets exhibited, what music we listen to, what movies get produced, and who attends the museums, concerts, movies, and plays. Money influences who goes to which schools, the quality of education we receive, and how much education we have. In large part, it determines who gets elected to public office, what legislation passes, and who does time for breaking laws. And the list goes on and on.

Our culture has a love-hate relationship with money. We love it for the power and things it can buy, and we hate it for the power and things it can buy. We constantly judge it as good or bad—for how much we have or for how it's operating in the world. There's very little we're neutral about when it comes to money. Just as in our personal lives we may both elevate or demonize money, we also elevate and demonize those who possess it or those who don't. Both extremes are a result of the powerful invisible aspects of contemporary culture that swing wildly between the fantasies of money and of its moral meaning—that those who have it are superior/inferior and those who don't have it are inferior/superior.

Because we really don't talk about money and our relationship to it, we don't have a sense of what a "normal" relationship to money might be. We don't know if our family, friends, or neighbors count their pennies, are awake in the middle of the night with terrors about money, make charitable contributions, can no longer afford to purchase their medications or feed their dogs, and so on. We know from our own lives, our friends' lives, or from the news that there are terrible realities to face about money in our world. We feel the increasing economic insecurity as the gap between rich and poor widens, as jobs are lost, and as the number of safety nets within families and society decrease. We also know that money is unfair, that there is oftentimes no rhyme or reason as to why one person is wealthy and another poor, or why someone works hard to barely make ends meet and another works just as hard and is remunerated exceedingly well.

Things, Things, and More Things

We have more material wealth than any society in human history, and yet we are far from satisfied. No matter how much money or how many things we have, most of us want more. We buy, for so many reasons, including because we crave the feeling of acquiring, we succumb to peer pressure, we want to improve our self-image, something is useful, we want to be in a better mood, or it is a good value for the money. What would seem quite insane in most other cultures is perfectly normal behavior in ours: when we don't have room for all our things, we either move to a bigger home or rent a storage unit to store them in.

In his book *The Gift*, Lewis Hyde writes that in a market society such as ours, the things of value are those that have a "public currency." Gifts and talents, both inner and outer, that are not of worth in the market place gain us no recognition or value. It is acquisition alone that empowers us, " . . . getting rather than giving is the mark of a substantial person, and the hero is 'self-possessed,' 'self-made.'" And if things are what give us substance, then of course, we want, perhaps even need, more of them.

Homo sapiens have always used and acquired objects. We are attracted to an object for itself, for its usefulness, or for some quality it embodies. Objects can be seen as extensions of ourselves. And they can also be a symbol of money or wealth. Objects and money are symbolic twins.

We are constantly bombarded by images showing that money, and the things it can buy, will bring us health, happiness, beauty, and a carefree life. Perhaps it's not surprising, then, that most of us secretly believe happiness is just the next purchase away, or the next, or the next. . . .

It's no wonder that consumerism has become the major activity of our society, as it combines both our society's near-obsessive focus on money, its ideal of individualism, and our very human need for objects of our own. Sharing does not enter the equation. Why? Because not only does sharing mean relying on others—something contrary to our culture's individualistic notion of self-sufficiency—but it's also not good for the economy. Advertisers increasingly target younger age groups in an effort to develop future consumers who will crave their goods and believe their message that happiness is about consuming and is just the next purchase away. And for the majority of us, buying for ourselves is more thrilling than borrowing from a neighbor. We grow more and more isolated in our consuming as we shun relying on others and avoid the human connection that comes from borrowing, loaning, and working together. What consumerism gives us in personal thrills actually limits the ordinary nourishment we derive from mutual sharing.

The movement toward consuming fewer things is inspired by environmental concerns and by our having less disposable income, as well as the current economic instability. It's not easy to change our consumer habits and our sense of entitlement, but many of us are slowly shifting our expectations about what we must have. Some of us are pushed to change more radically due to job loss or reduced income.

Olivia lost her very well-paying job in her midthirties:

For two years I didn't have any income and lived off of my savings. I recently started working part-time and I love the money I earn. I have a much deeper respect for money than I used to and would certainly never take it for granted again. And it has far more value to me than its financial worth—it has also become a symbol of my return to the working world.

But money is still very tight and I've depleted my savings, so I am extremely careful with it. Everything I buy is based on true need, not on want. Even when I'm shopping for food, I ask myself do I really need this avocado or this bag of cherries? Occasionally I treat myself and go treasure hunting at the local thrift store. My experience of having no money has left me with huge empathy for all the people in the world who struggle for economic survival, and I realize the difference we can make to millions of people by buying products that are fair trade. So I don't buy anything—tea or coffee or bananas—unless it has organic and fair trade certification. Then I feel that my precious money is being doubly well used, benefiting me and the people who make the things I consume.

A lack of money has made me very aware of the difference between wants and needs. I actually need very little and over time the 'wanting' has died away. I don't long for new clothes or new stuff of any kind. Shopping has lost its allure and there is such freedom in this.

Questions to consider about cultural influences:

- What three things has the culture you grew up in taught you or conditioned you to believe about money?
- Are you comfortable with your level of spending?
- If not, how would you like it to be?
- How do you react to advertising?
- What kinds of things are you seduced to buy?
- What things that you buy bring you the most pleasure?

Women and Shopping

As strange as it may seem now, in the first century of our nation's history, women were for the most part shut out of the basic activity of consumption: shopping in public. In the 1850s, Elizabeth Cady Stanton launched her battle for the rights of women—and one of those rights became the right for women to spend the family's money. Shopping was seen at the time as a way for women to become empowered by making decisions about purchases. Married women who could afford to were expected to stay home and have little public presence, so shopping provided them with both a means of being outside their homes and of having contact with other women.

Since the 1850s, women have certainly become empowered shoppers! Women now make 80 percent of the consumer decisions. Shopping is often seen as their familial role and civic duty, a source of consuming pride—both literal and figurative—displayed on mugs and license plate covers that read "Born to shop" and "Shop till you drop."

Shopping serves multiple functions in our society and in our individual lives. It still provides what Elizabeth Cady Stanton fought for, a means for us to be out in the world and to interact with others. It relieves boredom and loneliness by offering endless distractions, taking us away from ourselves with momentary activity and meaning. Shopping is a mechanism for self-soothing and for comforting ourselves, often compensating for feelings of being unappreciated, devalued, or neglected (either now or in the past). It gives us material goods that can make us feel more stylish, unique, special, and effective. It fills up the empty spaces of our homes with things, some of which are useful. It provides pleasure through making private spaces more comfortable, aesthetic, and distinctive. It brings an endorphin high, as well as well as a guilty and self-disgusted low. For some, it's a sport. At the same time, because of our conditioned desire to want ever more, shopping increases our sense of emptiness, isolation, and meaninglessness as well as our actual debt.

Louisa shopped compulsively. After each shopping binge she promised herself she would stop, but she couldn't. Both her credit card debt and confusion had grown very large by the time she attended a workshop. As she confessed, "I'll be at work, completely focused on an interesting project, when the thought of one of my favorite stores intrudes. The more I try to push it away, the stronger it gets. The longest I'm able to postpone my visit is for a few days. And I always end up buying a few things. I don't understand why this is happening to me. It's driving me crazy that I can't figure out why I can't stop shopping."

Louisa spent the entire day at the workshop compiling a list of possible reasons for her disturbing behavior. Perhaps it was connected to her having been adopted. Perhaps she felt guilty for being so accomplished in her career. Maybe she lacked outlets for her creative expression. And perhaps she was trying different identities—in order to find herself—through the various styles of clothing she was buying. She left the workshop with these ideas, and others, committed to determine the underlying reason.

About six months later we met for a session. She reported that although each of the hypotheses held a piece of truth, working with them hadn't brought any long-term change. As we talked for a few sessions she hit upon the reason which, once she saw and understood it, brought an end to her compulsive shopping. Louisa realized she had fallen in love with her boyfriend and saw that she was more dependent on him emotionally than she was comfortable being. Her secret overspending gave her emotional distance from him, providing an outlet for her anxiety about being so close with him. Seeing this, she began to acknowledge and work on her fears of dependency and commitment, and her overspending immediately stopped. If it sounds magical, that's because it is. It's not easy to hit the psychological nail on the head, but when you do, even long entrenched behaviors can change.

Ask yourself about:

- What are your role models for women and shopping?
- Who made the consumer decisions in your home when you were growing up?
- What advertising messages are you most vulnerable to as a woman?
- Are you comfortable with how much time you spend shopping and how much money you spend?

Nonmaterialistic Values

Although we are as a whole the most consuming culture that has ever existed, we are also a culture in which many of us look for ways to have interactions with others that are not dominated by financial transactions. We long for human connection that doesn't have to do with money. We are drawn to share our skills, time, tools, plants, and knowledge with others, freed from the impact of financial gain or loss. Many of us help by volunteering through nonprofit organizations and religious institutions. Or we assist in times of crisis, such as in New York after 9-11 and in New Orleans after Hurricane Katrina. Or we volunteer on projects working with the natural environment or with animals, some of the appeal being that trees and animals don't speak the language of money, even though their lives are so deeply impacted by it.

The explosion of interest in do-it-yourself building and home repair, as well as domestic arts and handicrafts and food gardening, speaks to our hunger for nonmaterial values. Spending money is largely replaced with doing it, making it, or growing and harvesting it yourself. The resurgence in homemade and homegrown has been further fueled by the economic downturn, the rising cost of safe, fresh food, and a desire to scale down on waste in particular and consumption in general, among other factors. But I think what sustains it is the nourishment that come from non-monetary-based endeavors, from doing it ourselves, rather than paying someone else to do it for us. We are nourished by learning new skills, enjoying our accomplishments, and forging new relationships with those with whom we share information. And unlike shopping at the mall, we are changed by these experiences that bring us pleasures and understandings. Part of the appeal of religious practices, nature, and intellectual exchanges are their separation from the commercial. We all need to cultivate nonmaterialistic values in our lives in order to balance the prevalence of materialistic values that surrounds us.

The question to consider here is:

- What things that don't cost money bring you the most pleasure?

The Economics of Our Time and Place

Often—and usually without realizing it—we size up people we meet based on many dimensions, one of them being money. We also learn to size up ourselves in terms of money, generally through comparing ourselves with others. We each have our own version of "keeping up with the Joneses." We compare what we have with what others have, or seem to have, to calculate where we fall on the continuum from poor to rich.

It's a well-studied phenomenon that our feelings about how much we have are greatly influenced by what others around us have. Those who grow up without many financial resources in a community of people with similar means, tend not to feel deprived. They have a very different experience than those who grow up in the poorest family in a wealthy neighborhood, continually aware of not having what others around them have. Studies show that the amount we earn can feel just fine until we discover that a coworker receives higher pay for the same job.

Another dimension that shapes our relationship to money is the state of the economy during the different developmental periods of our life. What was the economy like during our childhood, our young adulthood, working years, parenting years, retirement, and old age? Not only are our personal finances impacted by larger economic conditions, so is our view of money.

Questions about the state of our personal economy over time:

- Growing up, who did you compare your family with in terms of what you had?
- How did where you live compare to where your friends lived?
- What was the neighborhood like?
- Did you move frequently, and if so why?
- Who do you compare yourself with now?
- Do you feel social pressure to have certain items or brands?
- Are you ever concerned with "keeping up with the Joneses"?
- If so, in what ways?

FINANCIAL RESOURCES

How much money we grow up with influences our view of the world as a place where money is either available to us or not available to us. With new experiences, this perception can change over time, but these original conditions leave a large imprint on our expectations of what our lives and financial place in the world can be. Think about all the ways your socioeconomic class influenced what opportunities you had, what you were taught, who you met, who your friends were, where you went to school, what you expected your life to look like, and so on.

How we acquire our financial resources also affects our experience of having money. We generally handle it differently depending on whether it was earned, inherited, or a gift, and how it was made. How we feel about the money, our ownership of it, how active or passive we are in decisions about spending and investing it, the anxiety about taking risks with it, making charitable gifts of it, and our guilt or pleasure in having it are some of the main dimensions that are impacted by its origins and how it came to be ours. Marrying someone with money or having access to a husband's or partner's earnings feels different from money that directly comes to us through our earning it or inheriting it.

Our external conditions influence our identity and sense of self, but they do not determine it in any formulaic way. For some of us, growing up with the choices and indulgences of wealth can overwhelm our personal development so much that we are unable to develop a sense of self that is actually separate from money. The same can happen for those of us who grow up in poverty, with our sense of self being overly determined by a lack of money. Some are able to use the offerings and opportunities of wealth, or their lack in poverty, as a motivation and as enhancement of identity. Others cannot.

Laura did not let her humble beginnings get in her way or determine the direction her life would take. She became highly educated and is now a professional woman. Her colleagues never guess her background, and she does not reveal it to them. So when the occasional reference to white trash occurs in conversation, Laura shows no outward reaction, but her skin crawls with shame and anger. And occasionally when she is under stress, the despair of her impoverished past returns. There is no forgetting where she came from, and no need to. Remembering the little girl who felt so unprotected and powerless is important as she is still a part of Laura. It would only be a problem if Laura didn't also acknowledge all that she has accomplished.

Questions concerning socioeconomic status, past and present:

- Describe your family's financial status when you were growing up. Did your family consider itself to be rich, poor, or in the middle?
- Was there enough money?
- Were there changes in your family's socioeconomic situation while you were at home?
- Were you aware of differences in resources or socioeconomic class when you were growing up?
- If so, what made you aware?
- When did you first learn there were millionaires and billionaires, and what did you imagine or think about them?
- How did the financial resources in your family growing up affect how you live today?

IMMIGRATION

We are primarily a country of immigrants. So whether you immigrated recently, or it was your great-great-grandparents who did, you probably hold at least one story of immigration and money in your psyche. Juana came to the United States from Mexico when she married, her husband having come to work on dairy ranches several years before. An American citizen, she cleans houses for a living. Juana began her money memoir:

In Mexico, my father had a store and we owned our home. There were twelve of us kids and we all worked together to have a better life. We were happy—there was a good feeling from working and being together. When I came here [to the United States], I didn't speak the language, didn't drive, and we had no money. But I was never scared. Maybe it's because I'm not afraid to work. My grandfather told me I shouldn't be afraid of starting from scratch because everything will be okay. He told me, "No es facil [It is hard], but it will be okay."

It was really hard for me to just stay at home when the kids were very young, because I like to be productive. When Anna was two years old and her brother was older, I worked cutting grapes in the vineyards. It was more than 100 degrees and the grapes were sprayed with pesticides, but I felt better working. I could buy shoes and other things for the kids. The United States—it's very materialistic. If the things aren't necessary, it's okay with me if we don't have them. People have and have and have stuff, but that's not my life. I have the most important things— family and friends.

Juana's twenty-one-year-old daughter, Anna, recently graduated from a private college, a "rich school" as she described it in her money memoir:

Attending the college I went to made me realize there is a lot of money in this world and that I was poor. There were others who were feeling poor, too. The rich kids got whatever they wanted. They partied a lot. I worked hard. It feels better when you work for it than when it's handed to you. My parents encouraged me to go to school and worked really hard for me to go. My mother told me that she would work for twenty-four hours a day if she needed to in order to make it happen. I know the only time my mother was scared about money was when they were paying for my tuition. I received some scholarship money, but there was still a lot of pressure on them financially. I'm glad that I have a job now and help them out.

My junior year in high school I wanted to go on the school program to Italy. My parents asked me what's more important—to go to Italy or to go to college? I learned when it comes to money to think about what is necessary and important. I've worked since I was a sophomore in high school. I learned that all jobs are decent. My parents have always told us, "Never steal, have respect for other people, and have respect for yourself."

Immigrants come to the United States from all over the world with a similar strong work ethic and determination, whether they are fleeing poverty or political oppression. Some have sacrificed their professional identity. They seek a better life for their children, and sometimes, also for themselves. Their drive is to earn money to survive and often to help their families at home, but more so, it is for the freedom and opportunities that the United States offers. Immigrants, who often fill the lowest paying jobs, dream big for their children.

Questions about the influence of immigration on families and indivuduals:

- When did your family immigrate to the United States, and what were their economic conditions when they came?
- How does the story of immigration affect your views of money?
- If you yourself immigrated, what was it like for you?
- Did your economic status change?

RACE AND ECONOMIC STATUS

Race is one of the strongest indicators of economic status for women. Women of color and their children are the poorest of the poor. Women of color often fill the lowest-paying positions, and because they generally lack a safety net of family resources to fall back on, they are most vulnerable to downturns in the economy.

In *The Color of Wealth: The Story Behind the U.S. Racial Wealth Divide*, Meizhu Lui and her coauthors attribute the current vast differences in wealth among racial groups to a systemic problem of longstanding discrimination. The authors write that wealth in the United States is generally inherited, and families of color have not been in a position to bequeath wealth not only because people of color have traditionally filled lower-paying jobs, but for centuries, the authors say, they were "barred by law, by discrimination, and by violence from participating in government wealth-building programs that benefited white Americans." Government help for whites came through programs that few people of color were able to take advantage of, such as the GI Bill, VA mortgages, and being permitted to purchase houses with high resale value in good neighborhoods. Their children, moreover, have not had the advantages that many white families were able to provide: money for schooling, for a down payment on a first home, or help getting through a period of financial difficulty.

Current statistics show that for every $100 of wealth in white families, families of color have 16 cents.

The Color of Wealth reinforces that one's economic success is not often simply the product of individual attributes or striving—much has to do with access to opportunity, and that although race is not the only source of economic struggle, it is a significant one. Women of color experience the double discrimination of gender and race. In her study entitled *Lifting As We Climb: Women of Color, Wealth, and America's Future*, Mariko Lin Chang cites that median wealth among single black and Hispanic women is $100 and $120 respectively, while their same-race male counterparts have $7,900 and $9,730; the median wealth for single white women is $41,500. "To put it another way," the author states, "single black and Hispanic women have one penny of wealth for every dollar of wealth owned by their male counterparts and a tiny fraction of a penny for every dollar of wealth owned by white women."

A larger percentage of women of color, both married and single, have worked throughout U.S. history than have white women. And a larger percentage of those were mothers, often taking care of other women's children and homes. The ideal of women staying at home to tend to their homes did not apply to nonwhite women. Women of color predominantly worked as domestics, agricultural workers, and factory workers. They worked on the war effort during World War II. (Of course, the fifty thousand Japanese American women in internment camps were not allowed to join in, and moreover lost their family's property with little or no restitution.) Along with white women, the participation of women of color in the workforce soared in the 1950s, and new careers and positions opened to them after the Civil Rights Law of 1964.

History comes alive in women's personal stories. And each racial minority group has its own stories, of how it has been treated economically, both historically and currently, by the European Americans. The Native Americans' story is largely one of losses suffered. Patty, who works part-time as a college professor, shared part of her story:

Among Native Americans, success is not measured by how much you have but by how much you can give back to the community. I was raised to be frugal and to save money in case someone needed it, to believe that people take care of each other. It's important for me to have money for subsistence and for ceremonies. Everyone comes together for the ceremonies. Whatever you do and whatever you have, all are seen as equally important to the community, from fishermen to lawyers to teachers to health workers. Part of your responsibility as the ceremonial leader is to feed everyone there—whether it's 50 people or 750. I've asked lots of women how they would spend the money if they won the lottery. They all have told me they would take care of their family's needs first and then start a nonprofit organization to help Native American people.

Patty's tribe, and many tribes in the state in which she lives, were almost decimated by the greed of the early white settlers who took their land, and killed many through combat, alcohol, or the diseases they introduced. She told of picking berries in the summers with her grandmother and sisters by the side of the country roads. Each time a car approached her grandmother had them all hide behind the bushes. Patty later came to understand that her grandmother was trying to protect them, for when her grandmother was a teenager the white men in the community often raped the tribe's women as they were picking berries. Patty functions both in a white world that she sees through Native American eyes and in the tribal world that deeply nourishes her. She is well aware of the suffering of her ancestors and the blocks to full participation in the larger economic world that still exists today.

Questions to ask about racial attitudes and money:

- What teachings that you received about money do you tie to your race?
- What experiences have you had with money that were based on race?

MONEY SUPERSTITIONS

The ancient Greeks threw coins into their wells to keep them from going dry. Today, we toss coins into wells and fountains for good fortune.

If the palm of your right hand is itchy, money will come to you. But if you scratch it, the money won't come. If your left palm is itchy, it means you will have to pay for something—so by all means scratch it!

When you give a wallet or purse to someone as a gift, placing money in it, even a penny, ensures that the recipient will never be without.

It is said that money attracts money, so never leave your pockets, purse, or wallet completely empty and never completely empty your bank account. Always keep at least a coin or two with you.

When you find money, even if it's only a penny, it means you'll receive more money soon. If you are walking in the street and you see a coin or a bill, always pick it up as it will attract more your way.

A bee landing on your hand indicates that wealth is on its way to you.

Naming a child Penny ensures that she will enjoy good fortune throughout her life.

Carrying a penny wrapped in brown paper will help you avoid your debtors. Placing your handbag on the floor or on the ground guarantees that you will never have enough cash.

On her wedding day, a traditional bride would place a penny in her shoe to promote a prosperous life with her husband.

Writing with green ink whenever you can means profits will flow freely from your hand.

Start talking about money matters with other interested women!

CHAPTER 4

Women and Money

❧

> The king was in his counting house,
> Counting out his money;
> The queen was in the parlor,
> Eating bread and honey.

—"SING A SONG OF SIXPENCE," TRADITIONAL ENGLISH NURSERY RHYME

THE WORD MONEY COMES FROM the name of the Roman goddess, Juno Moneta. She was the protector of Rome, guarding over the finances of the Empire, and coins were minted in her temple. It is interesting that the Romans accorded such an important responsibility to a goddess rather than a god in a society that was highly patriarchical—that is, ruled by men. Moneta herself has been largely forgotten, but we unknowingly refer to her every time we use the word *money*. In countless other ways, the connections between women and money have been forgotten, neglected, or undermined.

"Sing a Song of Sixpence," a traditional English nursery rhyme written in 1784, shows us very clearly that money is the province of men. The king was in *his* counting house, counting out *his* money, not *their* money and certainly not *her* money. The king's accumulating and counting money is all that's deemed important. While the queen sits in the parlor, pampered and protected, at the same time she seems confined to a life of dependence and triviality.

For centuries, women were kept away from money, even when it was our own. This marginalization of women in the legal and public spheres of money contributed to our developing a strong interior relationship with it. We are different from men psychologically and biologically, which extends to our experience of money. How women feel and think about money in all its intangible aspects has been ignored and devalued, yet our feeling and thinking continue to play a crucial role in how we interact with money.

In this chapter, we will take a brief look at some of the ways we interact with money and how being female has shaped our inner money life. Nature and nurture are both at play as we cover money and gender, looking at valuing and devaluing, the masculine and feminine, the brain, and a history of women and money in the United States.

MONEY AND GENDER

We live in a world that has long devalued women. It's no wonder that feeling valued and valuing ourselves is perhaps the most instrumental aspect of our lives as women, affecting what we allow ourselves to imagine and undertake, as well as the dynamics in our relationships with others.

One way women are devalued in the world is financially; there are lots of ways women have been marginalized economically. We know all too well that women's dependent and subordinate economic state has contributed to our lack of skills in understanding how to work with money—if we weren't allowed to deal with it, how could we learn about it? Without understanding the basics of financial vocabulary, how could we even know what questions to ask? And why learn about it when you have no opportunity to use your skills? The dependency on men for all things financial also fostered feelings of incompetence, vulnerability, low self-esteem, depression, and fear. On a more material level, it has also contributed to hunger and homelessness. And our economic marginalization has left us more vulnerable to sexual, physical, and emotional abuse. Without the means to leave, for example, wives who are being emotionally or physically abused themselves, or whose children are, often feel they have little choice but to stay with the abuser.

One of our emotional strengths as women, our urge to please others and avoid conflict, serves us well as caretakers, but can also contribute to our willingness to subordinate to men's leadership—in family life, in business, in society. Nonrational and emotional intelligence have been devalued in mainstream culture, along with heart-based values such as empathy, generosity, compassion, and sharing that women often express. As a result, many women grow up with the belief that how they experience the world and express themselves is second rate to men's, and their feminine values need to be pushed aside if they are going to succeed in a "man's" world.

Although this chapter addresses issues that have affected all women, please explore your own thoughts, associations, memories, and feelings as you read. Consider the circumstances of your female lineage—your mother, grandmothers, and great-grandmothers—and how the experience of your female forebears with or without money might have filtered down to you. We each have a rich, complex inheritance full of resilience, success, pain, sacrifice, disappointment, hardship, privilege, sacrifice, sharing—you name it—about what it means to deal with money as a female.

General questions about gender:

- What messages did you receive about being a woman in relation to money—making it, spending it, saving it, sharing it and giving it away, investing it?
- Were you treated differently based on gender in your family from your male siblings?
- What messages did you receive from your parents, family, community, ethnic group, race, and socioeconomic class about women and money?

THE FEMININE AND MASCULINE OF MONEY

A primary influence on how women relate to money is society's primary focus on masculine principles and its frequent dismissal of feminine principles. Feminine and masculine principles describe ways of being, thinking, organizing, and behaving in the world. These patterns of behavior underlie human activity, both individually and culturally. These principles are embodied in both men and women—that is, men may embody some feminine principles and women may embody some masculine ones—although women are more likely to express stronger feminine principles and values and men stronger masculine ones.

To get a sense of what I mean by masculine principles and feminine principles consider the following series of descriptive words for each. Rather than focusing on each attribute or word on its own, let the totality of the words and their meanings build and resonate in your mind.

Masculine Principles

Independence	Rational	Domination
Autonomy	knowledge	Mastery
Reason	Action	Assertiveness
Order	Doing	Aggression
Rules	Initiative	Boundaries
Regulations	Separateness	Separation
Hierarchies	Competition	Discrimination
Intellect	Goal-directedness	Systematization
Objectivity	Product	Science
Decisiveness	Outcome	Government
Judgment	Linearity	The law
Analytic thinking	Technology	

Feminine Principles

Interdependence	Instinct	Chaos
Connection	Caretaking	Receptivity
Relationship	Caring	Yielding
Community	Nurturing	Passivity
Emotion	Gestation	Spirituality
Compassion	Transformation	Awakening
Values of the	Nature	Participation
heart	Play	Process
Being	Imagination	Responsiveness
Generosity	Intuition	Insight
Sharing	Flow	Awareness
Mutual benefit	Spontaneity	Merging
Trust	Not knowing	No boundaries
Irrational	Unknowable	Knowing through
Unconscious	Unexpected	experience

From these descriptors alone, we clearly see that money in our culture is most often associated with the so-called masculine principles of individualism, position, mastery, and power. Because, historically, men have controlled the money and developed the systems to deal with it, it makes sense that they would systematize it in primarily—perhaps exclusively—masculine terms: as a rational, material science. And that the masculine aspects of money would be the most valued.

Let me say again that we're talking about principles, or approaches to money. Although women are more likely to act out of feminine principles and men out of masculine ones, there's no way to generalize about how all women (or men) deal with money because individuals are a mix of these qualities that are our human inheritance. We learn to emphasize and expand certain qualities and de-emphasize and ignore others, based on the nature we are born with and input from others and the society. Of course, we are influenced by the privileged position the culture gives to the masculine and its devaluation of the feminine, in both men and women. But no matter what our gender, we can have both feminine and masculine qualities. Needless to say, some women operate more from masculine principles with money and some men have more of a feminine relationship to it.

When money is at the center of a society, as it is in ours, dealing with money rationally, systematically and materially is not only essential to managing it well, but essential to our survival. And many of us directly benefit in innumerable ways from our culture, placing such a high value on material success—through a high standard of living fueled by innovation and invention.

But dealing with money from a purely rational, individualistic model in which maximizing profit is the main goal, means our economy has worked extremely well for a few and not very well for many. Consider these hard facts: the top 1 percent of the U.S. population owns 40 percent of the nation's financial wealth, while the bottom 80 percent own only 9 percent of the wealth. In 2010, the average CEO earned 350 times more than the average worker. So natural does our economic system seem that few of us can even imagine more equitable or just economic conditions, let alone believe they could exist. This kind of individualism, which encourages greed as a by-product, can foster a disregard for the common good, often with devastating consequences, as we are seeing, for people and the planet.

Dealing with money as something that is external to us allows money to develop in ways that dominate our lives. As Jacob Needleman, in his book *Money and the Meaning of Life*, observes, "The conditions of modern life bring emotions of many kinds, thoughts of many kinds; but none of this fulfills us deeply within ourselves. Our feelings and thoughts about truth and value are pale when compared to the needs and sensations delivered to us by the outer world. **We do not experience the inner world as vividly as the outer world.** All our vivid emotions are tied to desires and fears dealing with the outer world. Our feelings for God, for Being, for Truth—whatever we choose to call the ultimate unity of reality—pale when compared to the stimulations that survival and functioning in the outer world evoke. **Money, being the principal means of organizing and ordering survival in the outer world, thus seems the most real thing in our lives.**"

So money becomes what is real, and other aspects of life, such as love, friendship and even soul, pale. Part of the reason this has occurred is our devaluing of the feminine principle with regard to money—a principle that values sharing and caring. Within contemporary culture, the feminine principle is considered at best naïve and at worst self-destructive when it comes to money.

But we need both the feminine and the masculine perspectives when it comes to money. As Carol Flinders states in *Rebalancing the World: Why Women Belong and Men Compete and How to Restore the Ancient Equilibrium*, "If it's a society we're constructing, that society must accommodate the whole range of human truths and human types—the fact that we are, for instance, relational *and* ambitious, reverent *and* innovative, idealistic *and* pragmatic, playful *and* industrious."

To use a money analogy, seeing money only from the perspective of rationality is like thinking you know what a coin looks like by looking at just one side of it. But when we look at the other side—when we start to give the feminine aspects of money equal value with the more material and concrete aspects—we will be able to create more health, balance, and wholeness in our relationship with money both individually and as a society. Decisions based solely on economic concerns will never be fully satisfactory, even if they give us money in the bank. Solutions that don't include our emotions, relationship needs, and concern for others, even if they're the best financial decisions, always cost us in other ways. The most common example is to become consumed with work, out of the choice either to get ahead or to make more money, without seriously considering the impact on our families and relationships. The neglected feminine side of money needs attention.

For most women, money represents a means, not an end. It is not the money or even what it signifies that they are after, but what they can do with it. They use it to take care of themselves and others, they share it, give it away. It provides security as well as adventures and experiences. More often, it is intertwined with relationship.

For many men, on the other hand, money is an end more than a means. It represents power and position. It plays out in terms of accumulation and competition. Men use money to compete with one another, to show off, to assert their masculinity and power, and to establish stature in the society. Donald Trump described this version of masculinity succinctly, "Money was never a big motivation for me, except as a way to keep score. The real excitement is playing the game."

Former Secretary of Labor Robert Reich recently confirmed this sense of the ways that men and women relate to money differently. Because of his position as an economist, social commentator, professor, and former cabinet member, I trusted the depth and breadth of experience Reich brought to our conversation about money matters. When I asked him about the male perspective on money, he said, "The business pages are all about deals, not about what the deal is for or what it will do—changing products or people. They're just about making money. This kind of disembodied conversation makes sense to men. It is an intuitive knowing for them, to accumulate and spend and gain a competitive position. But for women," he went on, "money is meaningful only in terms of what you do with it and in terms of relationships. The deal makes little sense to them. It's like trying to study Euclidean geometry without any sense of what it pertains to. The simplistic way of putting it is that for men money is about power and position. For most men, this is very obvious and there's no ambiguity. For women, money is more ambiguous."

That money is about relationship and about sharing for women is expressed by what Peggy Cabaniss, a financial planner, described: "I have been as successful as many of the men I know in financial planning. However, their definition of 'what is enough' differs from mine in terms of taking money from our businesses. Many men I know take much more profit from their businesses than I do. I have determined, however, that I have enough money for my needs and that I'd rather hire additional employees, nurture growth among new financial planners, and share the wealth. Men and women many times are governed by different messages learned from early childhood. Men are taught that 'bigger is better' and 'more is better.' Women are taught to share, to nurture, and to take care of others. These early lessons are carried with us as we become adults, build businesses, and deal with our relationship with money."

As with the masculine side of money, many challenges come along with the feminine. Identifying these challenges help us know how to unstick ourselves when they bring us to an impasse. Feminine desires for inclusiveness and difficulty setting boundaries make it hard for women to have appropriate limits. This can lead us to the dark side of giving—giving too much or in ways that are damaging. The story about my mother who couldn't say no to my sister's entreaties for drug money, recounted in chapter 2, is such an example, one that is not so uncommon among mothers. Both my mother and my sister were damaged by my mother's continual overindulgence of my sister and her profound difficulty in attending to her own needs.

Another limitation is that the feminine principle can create a more chaotic approach to money matters. As opposed to the masculine principle of linearity and focus, women tend to collect information and feelings from a wide expanse, gathering a multitude of ingredients that get stirred into a stew of feelings, thoughts, and understandings. Figuring out solutions can, therefore, rarely be a simple process for us. "It's a woman's prerogative to change her mind" is generally a dismissive statement, implying flightiness, lack of certainty, and a lack of intelligence. But as women, we are pulled to include many facts and perspectives in our decision-making process, which can lead to an overwhelming amount of information to digest, as well as to rich, new solutions. So, changing our mind can be a reflection of the different options and solutions we come to as we sort and synthesize so much information on many different levels.

The richness of the feminine principle's capacity to bring many perspectives together is illustrated in the story of Marion Weber, a member of a wealthy family involved in philanthropy. It illuminates the differences of the masculine and feminine approach from the perspective of philanthropy. Marion became unhappy deciding where to give money based on grant applications full of facts and figures, a process which she found estranged her from others as well as from her wealth. She took a year-long sabbatical from giving away money, after which she experienced an intuitive insight that inspired her to create a new form of philanthropy called flow funding. She began by giving an equal amount of money to eight visionaries whose projects she had previously funded. She stipulated that they give away the money in ways that they each thought would better the world. The only requirement was that they come together with her each year in a circle to share about the gifts they had made and their experience of giving. Each participant was asked to describe what inspired, challenged, moved, and surprised them.

Flow funding is rooted in the feminine principle, as we can easily discern from the core values listed on the Flow Funding website: "Generosity, Trust, Discernment, and Community. We seek to develop a form of philanthropy that is Proactive (not passive), Intuitive, Effective, Open to Surprise, and Healing for Funders and Recipients." Marion states on the website, "The Flow Fund Circle became a relationship-based form of philanthropy full of inspiration and surprises."

Marion told me, "Gifting meant something to me when it became a shared discovery process. It has become a vibrant healing-arts form instead of a duty or job. I love trusting the donors I choose and not knowing where the money will go. I love learning from their inspirations, challenges, and surprises. I am moved and inspired by their intuitive and heartfelt funding at the grass roots level. The circle and the way in which it organically reaches out into the world have given us all a sense of belonging in the world which is effective and filled with mystery."

Before the circle and flow funding, Marion found that having money caused many difficulties in her life. She felt that many people saw her as an "icon" of wealth, projecting their feelings about rich people and wealth on to her. She was constantly asked for money for one project or another, one group or another, one individual or another. The giving circle, or Flow Fund Circle, profoundly shifted how she found herself being treated by others and how she felt about herself in the world. She became grateful to her ancestors that she had inherited wealth that she could put to such positive use. The giving circle gave her a sense of meaningful connection—both to the members of the circle she empowered as givers as well as to the people and projects they were supporting. Over the years, she has expanded the model in many creative directions, and others have adopted it for their own philanthropy. Applying the feminine principle to money not only transformed her relationship to money, but to her life.

BRAIN GENDER AND MONEY

Recent research in neurobiology has demonstrated that male and female brains are structurally and functionally different. This research has helped to explain previous "folk wisdom" characterizations of men and women's ways of thinking and being in the world. And though there is much variation among individual brains, several biological differences between men's and women's brains help to explain differences between men and women's relationship to money.

These neurobiological findings support what we observe about women and money: that we seldom see ourselves and therefore our money in isolation, but instead as part of a web of relationships. That we have strong feelings for people and relationships, and these feelings need to be included in our decisions about money. That we compare ourselves to others, aware of what those in our circles have or don't have. And, that we can be concerned for strangers who are going without.

In her groundbreaking and highly acclaimed book, *The Female Brain*, neuropsychiatrist Dr. Louann Brizendine details the differences in structure between men's and women's brains. One important difference is that most women's brains have significantly more connecting brain cells than men's brains, which means they can hold many types of information at once, while male brains are wired to focus more singularly. Perhaps you've noticed, as I have, that it's often difficult for a man to do two things at once—like reading the paper and talking or cooking and helping a child with homework. (Once again I feel the need to say that neither the masculine nor the feminine are better than the other, they are just different. Multitasking is very important, but so is laserlike focused attention.)

Based on brain structure, a woman's thoughts and speech are informed by her sense of empathy, by bodily hunches—in short, by what we call intuition. A man's language skill, on the other hand, is more developed and tends toward an emphasis on linear thinking and facts and figures. And, the feminine brain is more amenable to change, and new cerebral growth, or what neuroscientists call plasticity. This suggests an ability to think about things from different angles and to incorporate new information more easily than male brains.

Brizendine takes brain differences between the sexes further when she states that not only structural but also chemical, genetic, hormonal, and functional brain differences between women and men lead to differences in how we perceive reality, and process thoughts, and in what we value. Communication, connection, emotional sensitivity, responsiveness, and empathy are all stronger in women because of how the feminine brain is built and functions.

Brizendine writes, "Under a microscope or an fMRI scan, the differences between male and female brains are revealed to be complex and widespread. In the brain centers for language and hearing, for example, women have 11 percent more neurons than men. The principle hub of both emotion and memory formation—the hippocampus—is also larger in the female brain, as is the brain circuitry for language and observing emotions in others. This means that women are, on average, better at expressing emotions and remembering the details of emotional events."

Brizendine writes that women's brains are wired to focus on the emotional reactions of others and to work hard at eliciting responses; a lack of response can make us feel that we are failing. Our brains, she says, are built for reading faces, hearing emotional tones in voices, and responding to unspoken cues in others. All babies are relational, desiring and responding to human connection. But newborn girls show more distress at the cries of other babies, and baby girls demonstrate immensely more facial gazing and eye contact than baby boys. She states, "A machine like that is built for connection. That's the main job of the girl brain, and that's what it drives a female to do from birth."

Brain research, according to neurobiologist Antonio Damasio, also shows us that reason and emotion are not the mutually exclusive processes we think of them as being. They actually work collaboratively. In an updated preface to his book *Descartes' Error: Emotion, Reason, and the Human Brain*, he states that when the book was first published in 1994, it met with some skepticism primarily because of its assertion that emotion is a part of reason and that emotion could assist the reasoning process rather than necessarily disturb it. In the 2005 edition, he said this thinking is now generally embraced in neuroscience. He goes on to say, "The reasoning system evolved as an extension of the automatic emotional system, with emotion playing diverse roles in the reasoning process. For example, emotion may increase the saliency of a premise and, in so doing, bias the conclusion in favor of the premise. Emotion also assists with the process of holding in mind the multiple facts that must be considered in order to reach a decision."

WOMEN AND MONEY—WHERE WE WERE

Moving from the female brain to women's history in America is an abrupt jump, but as we've learned from brain science, we're adept at making these kinds of leaps. And we're gathering information from all sorts of sources, to help you get a broad understanding of money in your life.

Whether your family's roots are in this country or another, the history of women in America affects you. When the United States was settled, men and women often worked together on the farm or in home-based businesses to produce what the family used, with little separation between their work and their home lives. The original colonies were small and very poor, necessitating a communal ethic. Before marriage, in all but the homes of the wealthy elite, daughters contributed to the family economy according to the sexual division of labor, working in family businesses, taking care of the household, and laboring in the fields. With marriage, a woman's duties as an economic partner were signified by the term "helpmeet" and "goodwife." Religious teachings and the laws of the land held that women were to obey their husbands.

Men were the decision makers and heads of the households. Their wives belonged to them. Anything a married woman owned, inherited, or earned belonged to her husband. When she married, she lost all economic independence and her legal rights were subsumed by her husband's. She could not sign contracts or sue for damages or divorce. And if she did separate from her husband, she had no right to the custody of her children. This legal doctrine called coverture (a woman was called *feme covert*, or covered woman), which followed British common law, lasted in most states through the nineteenth century, and aspects of it even longer. Husband and wife were one person in the eyes of the law—and that one person was the husband. Economic dependency was codified in law. Only single or widowed women could own land or a business, keep their wages, or sign contracts.

In the eighteenth century, as the former colonies became a young nation, communities grew into towns, and the market economy developed. The self-renunciation of the Puritans fell away, replaced by individual self-preservation and initiative. Religious and cultural institutions taught that each male (read *white* male) was to fend for himself and his family, acquiring wealth, knowledge, and material possessions. Economic independence and achievement were seen as signs of God's blessings. By 1787, women, who initially had been permitted to vote during colonial times and early statehood, were prohibited from voting (in all but one state, which later disenfranchised women). Women regained the right to vote in federal elections 133 years later in 1920, when the nineteenth amendment became law. The struggle for suffrage had been a long one; it was first seriously proposed in 1848 at The Seneca Falls Woman's Rights Convention.

In the nineteenth century, the Industrial Revolution took men and single women away from working at home and into wage-earning jobs, primarily in factories in towns and cities. The goods made in the factories supplied what had previously been made in the home and for the economically privileged, a new role developed—that of the consumer. By the 1880s, clothing, food, furniture, housewares, and other goods were largely being purchased. Wives became responsible for buying, using, cleaning, and maintaining consumer goods, and advertisements were directed toward them. The home became the ideal and idealized place for women.

Economic development and the ideas of the Enlightenment fostered numerous reforms during the 1830s and 1840s, including a movement for women's rights. Women organized in homes, churches, and social clubs. Mississippi passed the first Married Woman's Property Act in 1839, granting property rights to married women. The law was inspired by a state Supreme Court ruling that held that a Chickasaw woman could protect her property from her white husband's creditors because Chickasaw tradition granted married women independent property rights. Women held roles of economic responsibility and influence in many North American Indian tribes as well as in the areas colonized by the Spanish. At Seneca Falls women sought to correct inequities in family relations, including rights to control property and wages as well as guardianship of their children.

The end of the nineteenth century was a time of much change. The Victorian emphasis on character—a kind of moral toughness and integrity based on hard work, self-sacrifice, and frugality—changed into a focus on personality. Social performance became the key to wealth and power. Personality was evaluated on poise, charm, grooming, health, and the development of unique personal qualities that attracted others. These qualities were often attached to consumer items. Women were often dependent on men's wages to purchase the items now seen as so necessary to a happy existence.

In the twentieth century, as the nation recovered from the Depression, money became even more important. The field of advertising grew ever more powerful, assisted by the field of psychology, in promising a greater sense of well-being and prosperity through consumption. Health concerns were tied to products, with wives being chided for not properly feeding the children or perfectly washing the bathroom.

For a century, advertising has feverishly insisted that women are inadequate unless we buy the latest widget or whoozit, or look a certain way. These pitches help create a sense of inadequacy about our very being, a feeling that there is something terribly wrong with us. And that money, used to acquire the appropriate products, can make us whole.

Historians recognize World War II as the watershed event in shifting cultural attitudes about white women's employment outside the home and women's attitudes about their rights to equality in the workplace. During the early 1940s, women entered the workplace in larger numbers than ever before, both to replace men who had gone overseas with the military and to step into other jobs newly created for the war effort. Married women's participation in the workforce had grown slowly in the decades before, but shot up to six million at the height of the war. While the industrial demand for their labor receded after 1945—and in fact women were urged to leave the workplace to make jobs available for returning soldiers—a great many women stayed on as full-time or part-time workers to fill jobs in manufacturing and the new pink-collar sectors of office work and retail. By the 1950s, one in three women worked outside the home. Through labor organizations, these workers brought the first challenges to inequitable pay and sex discrimination.

Nonetheless, vestiges of coverture remained into the 1970s. In most states, married women were not legally able to establish a business without their husband's permission or to get credit or buy real estate in their own name without a male cosigner. The Equal Pay Act passed by Congress in 1963 was the first federal law addressing wage differences in compensation, though it has not yet achieved equal pay for equal work. Title VII of the federal Civil Rights Act of 1964 guaranteed equal opportunity to employment. At the last minute, the word "sex" was added, extending the bill to forbid job discrimination on the basis of race, religion, national origin, *and sex*. Extending women's rights further, Congress passed a ban on sex discrimination in lending in 1974. The Equal Rights Amendment, introduced in 1923 with the language (in its entirety), "Equality of rights under the law shall not be denied or abridged by the United States or by any State on account of sex," wasn't passed by Congress until 1972—and then fell three states short of ratification in 1982. It has not been taken up since.

Until not all that long ago, most women who worked outside the home did so out of necessity. Even so, their incomes were often trivialized as "pin" money to supplement their husband's earnings. Lisa, a teacher, minimized the value of her financial contribution, explaining that she and her husband used the money she earned for dinners out and vacations, while her husband's earnings paid the "real" bills. In the 1980s, women were not only working, but also were thinking more and more in terms of careers. As challenging work became more available to women, working became more attractive and socially acceptable. Women began attending law and medical schools and became policewomen and politicians in significant numbers.

Lesbian Couples and Money

Same-sex couples pay dearly for being life partners rather than married couples as they are denied the numerous financial and legal benefits that married heterosexual couples receive. One enormous way they pay is through inheritance tax because there is no joint property and the only gifting permitted tax free has to fall within the annual gift tax exclusion. In terms of Social Security, same sex partners are not entitled to the option of taking a percentage of their partner's social security benefits if they are higher than their own, a benefit that legally married couples receive. Additionally, they aren't entitled to the widow's survivorship benefits.

There are lots of other financial losses for same-sex couples, some of which concern: joint filing of tax returns, child support, retirement savings, pension, estate and gift benefits, bereavement and sick leave, and Medicare. Only some states recognize domestic partnerships. According to the Kaiser Family Foundation, only 36 percent of large companies that offer health benefits to their employees provide coverage for same-sex domestic partners. So if a woman lives in the right state and works for the right company, she can provide health coverage for her partner. However, employer benefits for domestic partners are considered taxable income. So she will pay tax on the coverage her partner receives, based on the cost of the coverage to her employer, yet another cost that married heterosexual couples do not have to pay.

WOMEN AND MONEY—
WHERE WE ARE TODAY

Women now control more than half of the private wealth in the United States! And we now comprise more than half of the workforce. In the most recent decades, women's incomes have become significant in both our personal and our national economy. Especially as it now takes more than one paycheck to sustain a middle-class family lifestyle, just as it long has for working-class families.

Today, working wives bring in 45 percent of total family earnings, and more than 22 percent of women between the ages of thirty and forty-four earn more than their husbands. Increasingly, married women are becoming the sole breadwinners. And women are projected to fill more and more jobs in the future, from blue-collar to middle management. Nonetheless, women continue to earn substantially less than men for similar work: 81 cents to each dollar earned by a man for comparable full-time work. This figure has changed very little over the years. For this reason, and because women still tend to hold lower-paying jobs and be in less lucrative careers, they have far less in savings than men. And they are more likely to have intermittent employment patterns and jobs that don't provide employer-sponsored health or retirement plans. (Only 3 percent of Fortune 500 CEOs are women.) After a divorce, women are more likely to see their standard of living slip than are men. More women are single heads of households than men. More women than men live in poverty.

A study by the American Psychological Association in 2008 found that money and the economy topped the list of stressors for 8 out of 10 Americans. (The survey was conducted throughout the year but the last of the data was collected just as the stock market was plunging.) What's most pertinent is that their findings showed that women are most likely to report feeling stress about finances. More women than men reported being stressed about money (83% vs. 78%) and the economy (84% vs. 75%).

Women have more economic power and have become more active in relationship to money, but we haven't changed the "face" of money yet, meaning money still functions pretty much as it always has, with men still the major players in the financial arena. Despite heartening statistics about how much wealth women control and earn, we haven't emerged very far from the Dark Ages, yet. Huge corporations, financial firms, and banks—most run by men—determine the economic lives of the majority of us. Their agendas are to make the most money they can, often without concern for the well being of anyone or anything besides their executives and shareholders. We don't have to look too far to see plenty of evidence of inhumane practices, greed, and misrepresentation in all industries. Look at the enormous profits the mortgage lending industry gained by irresponsibly approving loans, with no regard for the consequences in the borrowers' lives. Look at the priorities of government, bailing out the banks while individuals lose their homes or the decades-long practice of using the social security fund to service our country's debt. Or the "pusher" banks that give young people just starting college multiple credit cards with free backpacks or T-shirts for signing up. And there's the drug of choice for many of us, "free" miles, which the merchant actually ends up paying for. Some people are making extraordinary profits, but for the majority of people, it gets harder and harder to put food on the table, have two cars, a home, and pay for medical care. Our standard of living is declining fast—many of us are falling into poverty. None of it's a pretty picture—and there's not much evidence of feminine principle values.

Yet as we continue to gain greater comfort and familiarity with money, and are increasingly less dependent on men for our financial survival, I believe we have a greater opportunity to have an impact on our perceptions and views of money, individually and societally. We desperately need more heart-centered, nurturing, and humane attitudes toward how money operates in our culture. The place to start to do that is in our own lives. So the rest of this book returns the focus to your relationship to money.

Questions regarding the gender economy and how it has affected you specifically:

- Do you think of money as being either masculine, feminine, or both?

- What messages did you receive from your parents, community, and family about being a woman and making (spending, saving, sharing, giving, investing) money?
- How has being a woman influenced your experiences with money, work choices, and income?
- Who were your female role models for earning money?
- What did you learn from your female role models about earning, spending, sharing, giving, and investing money?
- Has being a woman influenced your experiences with work choices and income level?
- How is it different for you to negotiate a money matter with another woman versus negotiating with a man?
- Have you felt you were treated differently regarding money in either the workplace or by financial professionals because of being a woman?
- If you have children, how has money impacted your mothering?

exploring your emotions around money

Money doesn't have to be a mystery.

The more you interact with it, the more

your understanding and appreciation of it

will expand.

CHAPTER 5

Fear and Confidence

*I'm actually making enough money to raise two kids on my own. But the minute I
have an unexpected expense, I begin to imagine myself as a bag lady.* —ANDREA

M OST WOMEN EXPERIENCE FEAR WHEN IT COMES TO MONEY—fear
that we won't have enough money to survive as well as fear that
we won't know how to manage the money we do have. We may fear
that something terrible will happen and we won't be able to take care of
ourselves or that nobody will take care of us. We may be afraid because
we have lost our money, or afraid that we will lose whatever money we
have. And it's only natural to have fear during a financial crisis. Fear is
connected to feelings of vulnerability and uncertainty. So whether we
have money or not, these fears seem to be universal.

In this chapter, we will explore the inner emotion of fear as well as
the inner resources necessary to counter that fear, including confidence,
knowledge, and interdependence and connection with others.

FEAR PARALYZES—AND CATALYZES

Fear about money may have been in the air we breathed as children, in
the lives of others we observed, or in our experiences as adults. Perhaps
our parents' business failed or they developed a catastrophic disease.

115

Or we became afraid for our own well-being after driving by a hungry homeless child. Many things can plant a seed of fear within us as children. And when we became adults, the fear came from having a job and being afraid we might lose it or having trouble paying the bills. Perhaps our credit card spending was out of control or we lost money on an investment we made. The fear for our financial survival is intensified at times of divorce, illness, or the death of a partner or spouse—or from money lost due to business failures, economic conditions, or bad investments. In difficult financial times, many face extra burdens of assisting adult children, elderly parents, or other family members.

Besides the uncertainty of our individual circumstances, our fear is also linked to the uncertainty of our financial future, especially now that we realize how much it is affected by the national and global economy. Whether we live paycheck to paycheck or have millions invested, we are all vulnerable to economic forces that are unforeseeable and largely out of our control.

Some of this fear can be mitigated with knowledge. Those who are educated about finances, even just a bit, may have more confidence in reading economic indicators and be more comfortable with the rollercoaster ride of the market and economy. Those of us with little knowledge of these things often rely solely on the opinions of others, which makes us more vulnerable, especially as the information or advice we use to guide our decisions is often far from reliable or in our best interest. And without any knowledge, it is even difficult to assess the expertise of those we are relying on.

Reacting solely out of fear can cause us further problems. When we are driven mainly by a desire to alleviate our fear, the decisions we make may be not only impulsive but wrong for the particular situation. Yet, if we don't attend to our fear, letting it grow bigger and fill us with an inner darkness, we may become too afraid to act. That's why the common wisdom of "facing our fears" is good practice.

One source of our heightened fears is how our brains are wired. Louann Brizendine notes that men's stress responses are triggered by immediate, physical danger, whereas women's are triggered by more diffuse feelings and worry about impending catastrophes—the smaller things of daily life.

Feeling fear is distressing, but it can also be a potent catalyst in getting our attention, putting our focus on things we should be worried about. When it comes to finances, fear focuses and motivates us to take care of business and gives us the stamina we need to learn new things and face difficulties. Fear can be a signal, pointing the way to a situation, wound, confusion, or vulnerability that needs our caring and thoughtful attention. Fear tells us that we need to reach deeper inside ourselves to find inner resources and to reach further outside of ourselves to find other kinds of support.

TAMING OUR FEARS

Even though Andrea had no problems paying her bills or providing for her two children, her fear of the "bag lady" visited her frequently. She described it this way:

When my husband left me and then lost his job, I was anxious about being able to provide enough for the kids and myself. But with a few changes in how we were living, we could get by on what I earned. Even so, I wasn't used to being without the second income as a backup, so I was nervous.

It seemed to me that wherever I went, I noticed a homeless woman living on the streets. Any unexpected expense, as there always is, like a vet or car repair bill, and I wouldn't be able to get the image of the "bag lady" out of my thoughts. I knew that if we were ever in dire need, my parents would take care of us; we could even move in with them. I knew intellectually that I wasn't as financially vulnerable as lots of single moms, because I had that safety net. But I was still afraid much of the time. So I started asking the bag lady questions when she'd show up in my imagination and listening to what she was saying. She told me that she didn't think I could make it on my own. And she was warning me that catastrophe could strike suddenly, as it had in my marriage. After a few of these "conversations," I figured out that the bag lady, far from being a fortune teller of my financial life, was the voice of my grief over the ending of my marriage and the voice of my fears of being on my own again and completely responsible for my kids.

Once I was on to her, I began a campaign to change my attitude. I took every opportunity to remind myself that I could take pride in having survived hardships before, that I was resilient, and that I could find my way after the divorce. I would literally talk out loud to myself about how good it was that I was able to provide for myself and the kids. I paid close attention to the bank statement when it arrived, feeling appreciation that I had a good income and that I was being so frugal. I accepted that, though I couldn't be sure of what the future held, I was doing everything I could to take care of myself and my family. I figured that nobody else was going to praise me—my parents were anxious about my making it and my ex was depressed about his own future. So I was the only one who could boot the bag lady out, and I did. It's not that all my grief and fear have gone away, but they come up when it's appropriate now, rather than at every little bump in the road.

The bag lady image, or some version of her, often visits women. She and her kin represent our fears about our survival, a powerlessness and vulnerability we feel financially. Like all powerful symbols, she represents a truth—in this case, the truth that we are all vulnerable and that events beyond our control can change our fortunes. Very few of us have enough wealth to be completely immune from becoming destitute, but far more of us worry about complete insolvency than need to. As women we have been groomed for generations to have insecurities.

Andrea had inner resources that were the right remedy for her fear. Many times we can reassure ourselves by taking action and/or by talking to ourselves more positively. Our inner messages to ourselves play a big role in managing our fear—and our emotional lives in general. We need to become our own confidence cheerleaders, supporting ourselves through difficult times as we would a friend who was afraid or taking on challenges. Figuring out the kind of support you need, and giving what you can of it to yourself as well as asking others for help, can be enormously reassuring. Such support makes it possible to go through the fear, learn from the process, and affect the outcome. It's okay, and often necessary, to be afraid for awhile, but there is no benefit gained from being too afraid for too long.

Experiences in the outer world can build up our confidence, making us less afraid. Though I didn't consciously choose to take the action that calmed my fears, it had that result. Growing up, I had always had enough money. Even once on my own, when I needed extra, a call home to my mother would provide. When she died—at the time I was returning to graduate school to become a psychotherapist—I used the money she left me to go to school and earn the hours toward licensure. Once I had a salary and income, there was always a financial cushion. And when I married someone who made just enough to support himself and contribute to raising his two children, we continued to use the cushion of my inheritance for the down payment on a home and unexpected large expenses until it was all used up.

Without the cushion, I was scared. I felt like a little girl who needed her mother to take care of her and keep away the monsters in the bedroom closet. My mother's money had always been in the wings, ready to take care of me, protect me, when I needed it. Until it was gone. The experience of being a helpless, scared little girl did not at all fit with my actual situation. So, I worked to understand my fears, tracing them back to early fears of the dark and of robbers under my bed, to my dependency on my mother, my general insecurities, and to my sister's life-and-death money dramas. I saw that there was a terrified, young part of me that hadn't ever stopped depending on her mother. Even after she died, the money she left me continued taking care of and protecting me. Without it, I felt abandoned. I had to learn to take care of myself in a new way and trust in my resilience and ability to handle whatever difficulties I needed to. Eventually my fears calmed down.

A few years passed, and seemingly out of the blue, my husband announced that he wanted to buy a bookstore in the small town where we lived. After some discussion, I agreed with his plan to use our home equity line of credit for the purchase. Over the years, he had periodically spoken of wanting to own a store, and it seemed like a good time for him to take on a new challenge and direction in his work.

We were both surprised that I didn't try to block his plan, as I had many times before with his entrepreneurial ideas. My emotional work with money was paying off. I'd come to see that I used money to stop myself—and my husband whenever I could—from doing things that brought up fear, especially fear for our financial future. This time I didn't apply the brakes.

Even though I hadn't intended to be involved with the bookstore, once we took ownership, it became abundantly clear that it would take both our energies if the store was going to survive. We had seriously underestimated the challenge. For the bookstore's first five years, I worked there whenever I wasn't working in my psychotherapy practice. I worked long hours, often into the late night. I reached deep inside myself to find the stamina and passion to work so hard. I developed new skills, including learning to work with my husband.

Working harder than I ever had worked before—both physically and mentally—gave me the sense that I had finally paid my dues for a pampered youth in which no kind of work, not even putting out the garbage or making my own bed was required because my mother did everything for me. And, using so many different parts of myself in the variety of tasks I needed to perform, brought me a new sense of security from having skills that could be of value in lots of settings. It brought a sense of confidence that being a psychotherapist had never completely provided. I was no longer afraid of not making it in the world.

The confidence in one's skills that comes from earning a living is something that some women with inherited wealth envy. There are many complicated emotions that come with inheriting money—and the fear of losing that money is one of them. Much as the money magically appears, it can magically disappear. Fear of managing it is another—as women who inherit money seem even less apt to have received instruction about finance than the rest of us.

Learned helplessness about money matters, acting as if one has no control or agency over one's financial life, is common to many women. Emily's story graphically illustrates how we cannot afford to be clueless about our finances, as well as how a lack of fear can get us in trouble. Any notion of financial limits was alien to Emily, a woman I met briefly years ago. She had experienced unlimited funds while growing up and inherited a sizeable fortune in her twenties. So it didn't register with her when her financial advisors began to warn her in her forties that she would run out of money if she continued her current rate of spending. It simply wasn't in her purview that money ran out. Their repeated warnings fell on deaf ears until she had absolutely nothing left. Only then did she become afraid, knowing how ill-equipped she was to get along in the world. When I met her, she was working as a security guard, living in a trailer on the construction site she was guarding. She regretted how oblivious she had been, for so long, to her financial situation. It was all very real to her now and she was very grateful to have a job and a roof over her head, realizing how close to homelessness she had come.

Emily was fearless about money because she was oblivious to her real financial condition and its limitation. Emily's story provides an example of how helpful our emotions can be—sometimes we need to embrace the fear so that we can respond to the danger we are facing. Fear can be a helpful signal that we need to wake up to danger. Like all feelings, fear is information. So it's important that we can feel it. Use the fear to figure out what's disturbing you in the current situation and whether fears from your past—real or imaginary—are also getting stirred up. Use it to learn what you need to support yourself through the difficulty, what the possible solutions are, and what actions you need to take in order to resolve the dilemma. Sitting with your fear can reveal a great deal. The stories that follow will illustrate how confidence, connection, and knowledge help us to best respond to fear.

We also know that we can get too afraid, so that we just react to the fear rather than use it to help us process how best to respond. It's not at all good for us to make money decisions when we are too afraid, when we are gripped with fear. So you'll need to find ways, if you don't already have them, to distance yourself from your fear just enough to gain some perspective. That can mean talking to friends or writing in your journal about your state of mind. Getting exercise. Being physically held or just being in the presence of others can work to calm some of us, as does meditation or prayer for others. Reading the newspaper is what I do. By the time I've made it through the front section, my fears are generally put into perspective enough that I can work with them.

CONFIDENCE INSTEAD OF FEAR

Confidence is a major antidote to fear—not confidence that comes from being fearless or arrogant, but a confidence in our ability to find the best solution for us, to find our way through difficult decisions and conditions. This kind of confidence doesn't make all our fear go away, but it calms the fear and supports us in taking the steps we need to take. For instance, we may not know how to deal with not having enough money to pay our taxes or how to respond to adult children continually asking us for loans, but we can have confidence in being able to figure out how to proceed to an answer that works for us.

Amber, a chef, had started to act on her dream of having her own restaurant. She enlisted a variety of consultants to help her draw up a business plan. She attended classes and took advantage of all the free advice available to entrepreneurs. Much as she had thrown herself into learning her cooking trade, she threw herself into figuring out how to establish a restaurant. There were many periods of doubt when what seemed like a promising source of money didn't come through or the landlord of a property she was interested in renting either dismissed her or upped the percent of profits he wanted. She watched as male chefs with half her experience won high-profile positions or got funded to open their own places.

Each time a plan fell through, she would be disappointed, but then she would find the resilience to start afresh the search for money and a site, with renewed confidence and clarity in her vision. Meanwhile, she supported herself at jobs she disliked, fell in love, got married, developed her entrepreneurial skills, and worked on decreasing her personal debt and becoming more conscious of money. Eventually, Amber was able to open her own restaurant, and on her own terms:

> The money guys always dangled the carrot and made it sound like a great deal, like I'd just sign without looking at the numbers. They underestimated my intelligence. When I pulled out of one deal that didn't make financial sense, they said to me at the conference table, "Go ahead and vent," as if I needed to break down with them. Another time, one of the deal makers asked me how old I was and what kind of relationship I had with my father. I can't imagine they would have said any of that to a man. I have felt insecure dealing with the money-men who have so much and not having money myself. But I've gotten better at being just who I am. I learned everything I know about the business side of owning a restaurant on my own. I'm not sure how much of not being able to find a mentor or recognized by potential investors had to do with my being a woman and how much was being African American. I appreciate now that all those false starts helped me to hone my intuition and business sense so I was in a stronger position to deal with the challenges once I opened.

INTERDEPENDENCE AND CONNECTION

Another antidote women can use to handle their fears is interdependence and connection to others. We find support in feeling we are not alone, whether talking about our worries with a trusted other, asking for help, or paying for someone's services to help find solutions. Even just being listened to can calm our fears.

The ideal of independence in our society is based on masculine principles. In financially traditional marriages, the man was seen as independent and the woman as dependent. But if you think further about it, it becomes clear that a man's independence existed only if there was someone taking care of the children, providing meals, and creating a home. Thus, the unpaid work in the home by a dependent wife enabled and ensured that the husband could function independently in the outside world. If we include the wife's work as valuable and necessary, the *interdependence* between wife and husband would become clear.

So we don't have to do it all alone—and in fact it's impossible to do alone! Interdependence refers to relying on one another economically (though it may include an emotional reliance as well, it need not). The idea of interdependence acknowledges that we cannot survive without others paying us, supporting us, feeding us, nurturing us, and caring for us, as we in turn pay, support, feed, nurture, and care for them. Money circulates throughout the society—and the world—in a continuously interdependent flow; our lives are intertwined financially with the lives of many others, both strangers to us and those we know. I know this directly from psychotherapy clients who have paid me for my services over the years and from the bookstore where the money we need for the store's survival and to pay our staff and ourselves is handed to me directly by hundreds and hundreds of customers. And when shopping, I am very conscious of helping to support others.

Susan learned about interdependence when she became ill in her midthirties:

> For the first in my life I became really anxious about money when I was ill. I saw how much more difficult it was to manage on a single income, especially when that income wasn't enough. It was a constant, pressing fear. I realized how many people

in the world live with this gnawing fear, and I had a new found compassion for their plight.

I was progressively getting sicker and weaker, but the treadmill of rent and bills meant that I had no choice but to keep working. I knew I was on the edge of a precipice and finally I reached the point where I simply couldn't get out of bed anymore. I have never been more frightened. I had gone from having complete confidence in my ability to earn enough to the terrifying reality of not being able to earn anything. My immediate family were either unable or unwilling to help and if it hadn't been for one of my cousins who stepped in and said, "It's okay, don't worry, you can come and stay with me and I will look after you until you get better," I don't know what I would have done. Given how independent and self-sufficient I had always been, it was very difficult to accept his help, but I had no choice. And this has proven to be one of the great gifts of this illness. I have learned that I don't have to do everything on my own, that interdependence is better than independence.

KNOWLEDGE AS AN ANTIDOTE

Knowledge about money is another antidote to fear. Most of us are uneducated about finances, and may not receive trustworthy financial advice. Luckily there are more and more financial literacy resources available to women.

We don't need to know everything there is to know about money, which would be impossible, especially as financial markets get more and more complex. But, as with all things in life, even learning some elemental concepts and terms will make us less intimidated and afraid about money matters, let alone help us to make better decisions.

More and more of us are educating ourselves about finances. Sometimes, however, it takes an event to get us to become more knowledgeable. The death of a partner or spouse is the first time that some women learn about money matters. For Julie, it was losing all of her inheritance that inspired her to learn. She explained in her money memoir:

My parents had their money invested with a close family friend, Jake, for years. They never worried about the money because he always produced the funds they requested. Their account went from being a modest one to being enormous. They didn't know to doubt it. When my mother was dying she told me how happy it made her that there would be so much money to leave to the four of us kids when our father died.

My expected inheritance meant that I could choose to work on the projects I was most interested in, ones that generally could only pay me at my lowest rate. I didn't have to worry about saving for my retirement, or so I thought. Well it turned out that Jake had given my parents' money, unbeknownst to any of us, to Bernie Madoff to invest. So all of it, except for what my parents had already taken out, went to feed Madoff's ponzi scheme. It has broken my father's heart to have lost all of his money. He's had to move from the apartment he and mother lived in for years, and my sister is helping pay the rent on a very modest apartment for him. Yet he still can't bear the idea that his "friend" Jake actually knew there was anything unscrupulous about Bernie Madoff. But I say that at the very least, Jake lied all these years to us, giving us the impression he was making all the investment decisions himself.

I've gone through so many emotions about this. When the shock first wore off I had to take sleeping pills and anti-anxiety medication for awhile. Having the inheritance pulled out from under me caused me to feel incredibly vulnerable and anxious. With the passage of time, I move more and more into acceptance and dealing with what is. I'm still angry, but I see that I can no longer be blissfully ignorant about money. I'm wising up. I should have been charging more for my work all along, and I've raised my fees. I realized I need to learn about money, and I've started to read the Wall Street Journal. Even the little bit of new information I have makes me feel less like a scared victim.

Questions to consider regarding fear, dependence, independence, and interdependence:

- What are your fears and worries about money?
- Have you ever been visited by your version of the "bag lady"?
- Do you worry that you will not have enough or not be able to support yourself?
- Are you afraid of dealing with your finances or making decisions about money?
- If so, in what ways?

- And what are you afraid of?
- Which of your fears about money have you inherited and from whom?
- Do you know what helps you generally when you are afraid?
- Does that help when you have money fears?
- Do you have confidence?
- Where does it come from?
- How can you build it?
- Do you have knowledge about your money matters?
- Where did you learn it?
- How can you gain more?
- Do you have a sense of interdependence?
- If so, with whom?
- How can you foster it?

NAMES FOR MONEY

....

almighty dollar

bank note

bills

bread

bucks

cabbage

certificate

c-note

cash

chicken feed

cold cash

coin

currency

dinero

dollars

dough

folding money

green backs

green stuff

jack

legal tender

long green

loot

lucre

milk money

moolah

notes

pin money

plastic

pocket money

rhino

roll

skin

stash

wad

wampum

We all are "funny" about money,

no matter how much or how little money we have.

························

CHAPTER 6

Shame and Pride

✺

It was essential to my father that we looked like an upper-middle-class family. You didn't have to scratch too far below the surface, though, to see the truth. In fact just coming through our front door and seeing the lawn furniture in the living room told it all. —SHANNON

O F ALL THE EMOTIONS INTERTWINED WITH MONEY, shame is one of the hardest to tolerate. We go out of our way to keep from feeling shame, but it's unavoidable—especially in our relationship with money. During my first meeting with a new accountant years ago, something she said made me think that she didn't want to take me on as a client. My eyes welled up with tears. I felt so inadequate and exposed as I revealed my jumbled financial records to her that I was primed for her to reject me as a client. Seeing my distress, she quickly reassured me that wasn't the case. She later shared with me that almost all of her clients felt shame about their financial lives, whether about their assets, their investments, their record keeping, or their lack of knowledge about money matters.

Shame is the feeling that there is something wrong with us, that we are in some way flawed. Shame includes feelings of various intensities, from embarrassment to humiliation. It can come attached to guilt, disgrace, anger, and mortification. It includes feeling pathetic, ridiculous, criticized, and humbled. Shame has to do with connection and separation, exposure and hiding, power and weakness, and self-worth and self-denigration. Feelings of shame—from slight to overwhelming—are always evoked in situations involving competition, power, comparison, judgment, and disconnection. We can't control or anticipate when we will feel it.

I think women are especially susceptible to feelings of shame due to the long tradition of female subordination in Western and Eastern culture. Feeling there is something wrong with us, of being thought of or seen as "less than," is deeply imbedded in our psyches.

We can feel shame about either how much or how little money we have, or both. With a neighbor, we might feel shame for having too little, but practically the next minute we feel shame with a friend for having too much. Talking about our personal finances often causes feelings of shame because we're at once breaking the taboo against talking about money as well as exposing ourselves in an unaccustomed manner. The indirect and nonverbal ways that we share about money often indicate feelings of shame.

Hiding is a hallmark of shame. Almost all of us exhibit shame, hiding our personal relationship to money, rarely speaking of it; when we do, we are extremely careful about what we say, careful to create a certain image. We censor the impressions we give, we cover up having or not having money, we make excuses about it, we lie, we are silent about it, we keep money secrets, and we use plastic credit cards that conceal how much debt we have. Sometimes we even lie to ourselves, about how little or how much money we have or how much debt we're in.

In *Shame and the Self,* Francis J. Broucek viscerally describes the shame experience: "Shame makes us want to hide; we avert our gaze and hang our head in shame. Shame is so painful that we hope it ends quickly; we have no particular desire to reflect on it or talk about it, because to do so is to run the risk of reexperiencing it. Shame is somewhat contagious; it is difficult to witness another person's acute shame or embarrassment without some vicarious twinge in ourselves."

THE SOURCES OF SHAME AND MONEY

Why does money cause us so much shame? Looking at the psychological sources of shame makes it clear what a perfect partner money is, in our culture, for shame. Almost all of the origins of our shame responses involve our relationship with others. It is speculated that shame is both genetic, a part of us, as well as socially constructed and therefore arises out of other people's responses to us, whether actual, imagined, or anticipated.

We feel shame (or one of its cousins, such as humiliation or embarrassment) when:

- We feel judged by others in either a deflated or an inflated way.
- We feel vulnerable and exposed, that we have revealed too much.
- We feel too much distance between ourselves and others.
- We judge ourselves negatively, with the root of these self-judgments being an assessment of our unworthiness by another person or societal norms.
- We damage our bond with ourselves, betraying or killing off a part of ourselves.
- The intensity of our shame reaction can vary depending on the degree to which we admire others, care about them, value their opinion, need their approval, or want to develop a relationship with them.
- In terms of the shame that comes from a break in our bond with ourselves, the intensity depends on the extent to which we've betrayed or damaged a part of ourselves.

Shame from Being Judged by Others
The first source of shame—being judged negatively by others—has to do with what another or others think about us, or what we imagine they think. One such story of shame is Shannon's. It was essential to her father to be financially successful. So much so that, even though

he had not been successful, he made certain that he appeared to have wealth, renting homes in high-end neighborhoods, leasing fancy cars, and wearing expensive suits. There was little money left over for other things the family might have wanted and needed. Shannon never once invited her friends over to her house, as she felt ashamed for people to see how her family really lived. This was, of course, just how her father felt:

> *My father put everything into making us look like an upper-middle-class family. You didn't have to scratch too far below the surface, though, to see the truth. In fact, just coming through our front door and seeing the lawn furniture in the living room told it all. All the kids I went to school with were wealthy and I felt somewhat out of it because we weren't. My father wanted me to keep up the front that we had money. When a friend was talking about her vacation, I couldn't let on that we never went anywhere because my dad worked seven days a week in his store. So I could never be myself.*
>
> *I got a double whammy—I felt inadequate with my peers for not having what they had and not getting to be myself with them, and I also was convinced that Dad thought there was something wrong with my mother and me, otherwise why would he have to pretend we were something we weren't? Unraveling my growing up really helped me see where my low self-esteem came from as well as see how my dad's growing up poor had caused him to think money was the only thing that counted. I could then understand that his embarrassment about how we really were as a family had nothing to do with who I was, that it only had to do with money, which freed me of lots of negative feelings about myself.*

Shame from Feeling Too Exposed

We also feel shame when we feel too exposed, too vulnerable, or that we've revealed too much. I once told a friend how much I had earned in my therapy practice in the past year. It was a period when I was working on being more open in my life about money. We'd talked before about money. We had discussed money in our families. I knew what her hourly fee was and she knew mine. We were talking about money in some general way when she asked me, directly, what my income had been. It was around tax time, and I remember that I felt proud of having made more than I ever had before.

My friend was quiet for a few moments after I told her how much I had made, and then responded, "Is that all?" She did not reveal her income to me, and I did not ask her. After an awkward silence, she changed the subject. Her response revealed a competiveness in her that I had not previously been aware of, a need to feel superior at my expense. As is often the case with shame, I still have vivid memories of the incident, where we were sitting and how I felt, even though so many years have passed. My shame came from feeling not only that I didn't measure up, but that I had exposed too much information about myself. I had made myself too vulnerable in a situation that, as it turned out, was not safe emotionally.

Relationships are a bit of a balancing act between our need to share and be vulnerable in order to develop closeness with others, and our need to keep some things private in order to protect ourselves. Without vulnerability, there can only be superficial exchanges. Yet we also need to develop trust with another before we share sensitive matters with them. Clearly, I had felt trusting of my friend. But my feelings of shame, in this instance, alerted me to the fact that it was not safe for me to talk about money intimately with her. She was no longer a trustworthy confidant concerning money.

Since the display of our wealth or lack of it is one way we reveal ourselves to others, we are always at risk of feeling too exposed. Some of us hide how much money we have in an attempt to not call attention to ourselves. Others of us are embarrassed by our own needs for attention and admiration, and by how much we use money to fulfill those needs. We can also feel shame when we are not prepared to be exposed, as when someone asks how much we spent on a piece of clothing or jewelry or even our house and, caught off guard, we answer before thinking whether we'd be more comfortable not answering.

We often experience feelings of shame when we talk about money. Money is so frightening in our society and our personal lives, as we have been seeing, that to talk about it on a personal level is bound to make us feel vulnerable and ashamed. This is compounded by the shame we experience from breaking the taboo against talking, and our being unaccustomed to exposing financial aspects of our lives. Any sensitive topic that we feel shy or uncomfortable talking about can cause us shame when we begin to be more open about it. This kind of shame can lessen over time as we grow more familiar sharing about these topics.

Shame from a Perceived Threat to Our Relationships

Yet another source of shame has to do with perceived threats to our relationships with others. Shame is a signal of our having done something or of someone doing something to us that creates a distance that cannot be bridged. Shame responses can be triggered simply by situations that highlight the difference in our economic conditions. Differences in our financial resources can create a distance that sometimes cannot be bridged—especially when there is a lack of understanding about the other's financial situation. Shame can also be a warning that a social or personal boundary has been violated, something common to relationships with people of different financial resources from our own. We don't want money to get in the way of our connections with others, but it can.

For example, a friend served on the board of a nonprofit organization with people who had far greater resources than she did. Debra's expertise rather than her wealth was sought for that organization's board. Having become friends with several board members, she was frequently invited to join in dinners or drinks at restaurants after meetings. But this presented a dilemma for her as she was going through a period of greatly reduced income. At first she went along, ordering as frugally as she could, a house wine or an appetizer or a salad for her dinner, explaining that she wasn't very hungry. But because the group generally split the bill evenly on their credit cards, she ended up paying for the more expensive entrées that others enjoyed.

Debra felt shame as a result of being unable to afford to go out with these friends, but she was too embarrassed to tell them why. Calling attention herself, to what already felt shameful (not having enough money), seemed unbearable. The real problem for her, as she came to see, was *their* apparent obliviousness to her financial limitations. Even though they knew of her job status, they seemed to blindly act as if her resources were similar to theirs. In a way, it was tempting to continue to go along with them, pretending that she was one of them. But Debra decided she had to decline their invitations. She didn't want to increase her credit card debt even more and didn't like feeling invisible to them.

If only someone had simply asked her, "Do you feel like a burrito or a nicer dinner tonight?" Being offered a choice would have bridged the distance between them, graciously acknowledging the difference while reinforcing their connection. Debra wished for a more sensitive response from her board friends, of course. Yet she took an important step to diminish her shame by accepting her genuine limits and then acting accordingly. This gave her a sturdier sense of self and enabled her to feel less vulnerable in relation to her more well-to-do friends.

The kind of shame that comes from a perceived threat to relationships can occur in families, as well. Jennifer came from a large family, with lots of love and very little money. Though her father worked as a teacher, and had as many as three jobs at times, her parents had seven kids in ten years, so there never was enough money:

> Things got much worse after my mother got sick, and there was a very large hospital bill. We were going to lose our home and so they found a loan shark to cover the house, but after that we could never catch up. I started working at the age of fourteen, and all the money I made at my jobs, I "loaned" to my father. He was ashamed that he needed it and asked that it be a secret between the two of us. My mother would tell me I should buy a new dress for myself, without ever knowing I didn't have any money because I'd given it all to my father.
>
> The electricity was turned off or the car was repossessed, so we couldn't get to school, and I'd feel badly for him. He was a devoted father and adoring husband. He never squandered the money, it was just that it took a lot of money to raise seven kids and send all of us to Catholic school. I needed a car when I started college, to get from our house to campus and to my job, and so my dad signed the loan. I gave him the monthly car payments and only years later, when I thought the car was paid off, did I discover that he hadn't given any of the money to the bank. He'd spent it all on the family's expenses. He wrote a letter, full of his humiliation, apologizing to me. That was the first time I was angry with him and felt I couldn't trust him. But even then I eventually forgave him. I always felt he was struggling.

Given her attachment to her father, it was understandable that Jennifer couldn't tolerate being angry or critical of him for very long. Perhaps she felt, unconsciously, that if she provoked his shame further, their relationship could have been profoundly damaged. Her positive regard and empathy for him, maintaining her view of him as her "hero," protected their relationship but at a considerable personal cost. Jennifer later added, "Skipping to today, I think my shame around money comes from his shame. It's part of what undermines my self confidence."

Shame That Signals Damage to Our Relationship with Ourselves

We feel shame when we judge ourselves harshly and negatively. We feel shame when we do something that doesn't live up to the standards we hold for ourselves. For example, Stephanie was ashamed to tell her friends that she'd loaned her sister quite a bit of money to start a business. She wasn't sure if her shame was a sign that making the loan had been a mistake, or if it was a sign that she didn't want to look at her competitive relationship with her sister.

Stephanie's story reminds us that there is a shame that signals a break or damage to our bond with ourselves. We feel shame when we are dislocated from ourselves, when we betray or suppress an essential part of ourselves in order to fit in or be accepted, either in response to our own thinking or to the demands from others that we conform to their ideas of how to be.

Sarah, who came from old money, experienced shame from living a "faux life," as she described it in her money memoir:

> Class cancelled out any power or freedom I felt from having money because of my parents' expectations. Things that interested or excited me were considered socially unacceptable. For example, when I decided to take up acting, my mother said, "Once the Social Register finds out you are an actress, you will be taken out of it." She called me Tallulah Bankrupt. In her mind, what was really important was knowing your china patterns, having monogrammed towels, belonging to the right clubs.
>
> For me, having an upper-class background meant I couldn't be or do anything I really wanted. My parents had no idea how to mentor or prepare us for any aspect of life's realities. The shame of realizing I knew how to do absolutely nothing and imagining everyone else knew what I needed to know kept me from having any idea of how to get gainful employment. Whenever life would cause me to get hurt, I'd assume my mother was right and that I was doing the wrong thing.

Sarah's initial healing work revolved around coming to terms with the damaging effects of having alcoholic parents. Distancing from her mother's control freed Sarah of her chronic shame, as it allowed her to reclaim her own relationship with herself. It freed her to develop in a way that was true to herself rather than being the "faux" Sarah who her mother insisted she should be:

They were too busy socializing to parent me. The paid staff took care of me. This was the same way they had been raised. My mother taught me that I could never be too slim or too rich and that booze was great for cramps or for shyness, so it became the way I got through the faux life I was being trained to live. I've come to see that my mother's sole preoccupation in life is to spend as much money as possible in a quest to buy love and control her family. And gradually I've stopped attending family "business meetings" as I realized they were merely an opportunity for my mother to be surrounded by men while talking about the golden carrot we've been promised all our lives. I've stopped looking for her approval or money which has freed me to finally live life on my own terms.

SHAME IS A PART OF BEING ALIVE

Shame is a sign that we are human, alive, and living a related life. Feeling some shame, a tolerable amount, is a sign that we are taking risks and expanding our comfort zone in being honest, revealing, and connected to others. Uncomfortable as it is to feel, there are positives to shame. It humbles us and it connects us to our humanity and the humanity of others. We can learn a great deal if we can tolerate the feelings of shame we are having and work with them.

Feeling inflated, letting our egos puff up, can cause a shame reaction. You know the feeling if you've ever started to brag about something you are proud of accomplishing, but you get a little too full of one part of yourself and you lose touch with the whole of you—then the pride slips into false pride, which then slips into shame. Shame actually helps in these situations to keep us the "right" size. This feeling can also occur when someone sees you in an inflated fashion, imagines you are a superwoman because of the money you have. Shame can occur when we are objectified and seen as being more than we are—just as powerfully when we are seen as less than we are.

> One evening I walked past a darkened doorway where a woman and her sleeping toddler were nestled in an entryway. A shawl by her feet was the only sign she was begging. I continued on for several blocks thinking about her. I wondered about all the things that could have brought her to this state and imagined how bereft and insane I would be if it were me, living on the streets. Perhaps she was drug addicted, perhaps she had left an abusive relationship, perhaps there were a series of misfortunes, I couldn't tell. Feeling it was wrong not to help, I turned back and dropped some money onto the shawl. Her face was hidden.
>
> There was a subtle, nagging feeling of shame after I left the money. I searched for its source. My act of giving reinforced my identity as a "have" and her identity as a "have not." My gift identified me as financially secure, empathetic, and generous. It made me feel better, not better than her, but it gave me an inflated sense of myself, temporary as it was. This caused a shame reaction in me.

We each need to become acquainted with the shame in our lives—learning to feel it, listen to it, and discern when it is tolerable and when is too much. Too much shame is a sign that we are feeling overly exposed and not protected enough. To be shameless is to ignore the impact of our actions on our relationships with others. To avoid, deny, or ignore shame means that we have to severely constrict our lives and interactions. Shame helped Elizabeth find her right size:

> I could tell that my parents were living differently from the people who were working for us. I spent a lot of time in the kitchen with the nanny, cook, laundress, and cleaning woman, and their families who would all stop by to visit in the kitchen. I knew all the problems of their kids and families. My parents treated these women with great kindness and respect in all ways, including financially, and so they were in my life for a very long time.
>
> My mother never came in the kitchen. She hadn't grown up with wealth but once she married my father, she fashioned herself perfectly into an upper-class

woman and lived with no seeming awareness of the economic challenges and upsets of others. I guess I was all too aware. I was embarrassed by our fancy Park Avenue doormen, in their formal uniforms, and the fact of my mother going to a dress designer for all she wore.

What did I do to deserve having money? The shame and guilt I felt about having inherited so much money caused me to work laboriously at everything I've ever done. I loved my mother very much, but in the realm of work, I always identified more with the people who worked for my family. I feel that if you don't make it by your hands, that you shouldn't put your hands on it. Working hard and not feeling entitled to anything has served me well—and kept my shame in check.

HEALTHY PRIDE

One antidote to shame, and a by-product of working with our shame, is healthy pride. Shame is evoked when we are stereotyped, objectified, patronized, judged negatively, or oppressed. Healthy pride comes from being seen, and seeing ourselves, for who we really are. It also comes from being appreciated—not as a mother or a wife or a woman, not as rich or not rich—but as an individual person. Healthy pride comes from the acceptance of who we are, with an appreciation for both our inherent worth and our humility.

The year she divorced her husband, Isabelle received a Christmas gift from a close friend:

It was a beautiful wooden box and when I opened it, there was a check for a large sum inside. My friend has been generous before, treating me to things, but I was shocked and embarrassed to find the check. I immediately called her to thank her and to say that I couldn't possibly accept it. She asked that I sit with it and reconsider— she told me that she knew I could get by on my own, but she wanted me to have a bit extra to buy special things for myself and the kids. Money was really tight and though the idea of getting to buy some gifts was appealing, receiving the check made me feel pathetic. And going without was the strong thing to do—it felt better than the shame of taking the check. I knew how to go without.

As Isabelle talked with friends of hers about the gift, including the woman who had given it to her, she worked with her feelings of shame:

> I came to see the check not as judgment about my abilities, but as an expression of my friend's caring and support. I was judging myself as pathetic because my ex had left me and because I was so worried about money. The check pushed me to work through feeling pathetic, to feel worthy of the help and caring, and to feel a sort of pride from facing the hard times I was in. I accepted the check.

It was through experiencing and struggling with her feelings of shame, rather than pushing them away, that she was able to work through them. It appears that this allowed her to feel more connected to important inner aspects of herself and more connected to her very loving friend. This experience of secure connection, inside and out, can be described as being a healthy state of pride.

Another example of healthy pride evolving out of a shame reaction comes from Marissa, who experienced shame unexpectedly in connection with something that she'd felt was really positive—her daughter receiving a generous scholarship to a private high school:

> My husband died when our daughter was very young. It's been a source of pride to me that I've been able to support our family working as a hospital nurse. So I wasn't prepared for feeling the shame I felt when I attended the first parents' meeting at the private high school my daughter was going to. All the parents looked really wealthy and drove new luxury cars, and I drove a beat-up old one with more than two hundred thousand miles on it. In the parking lot I had a really strong feeling that I was out of place, that I didn't belong there. It took all I had to go into that meeting. I started parking several blocks away when I'd come to the school. It seemed to give me more courage to be myself if I didn't start out by comparing our cars in the parking lot and feeling so much less than all of them.

As a nurse Marissa was used to working with patients of different financial means, but she was in the position of power regardless of their economic circumstances. In the setting of the material wealth of the private school, with her daughter receiving a scholarship, she felt shame.

Marissa courageously extended herself with some of the parents because she felt it was important in order for her daughter to have a good experience at the school. Over time she came to establish strong enough relationships with several parents that it no longer mattered how much money they had. If our bond with others is strong enough, we can maintain connection with them—even in the face of shame—which can also contain our feelings of shame, and over time dissolve them. Marissa came to feel a healthy pride for who she was and for how her life was, including the car she drove.

Questions to think about concerning pride and shame:

- Can you think of a time when you felt ashamed for how much money you had, either for having too little or too much? Shame for the clothes you wore, the car you drove, or where you lived?
- In what ways do you feel shame about money now?
- Do you compare yourself to other women or men in terms of money?
- In what circumstances and ways?
- Do you feel shame and/or pride when you do?
- Have you or do you feel judged by others for what you have— or don't have?
- Do you try to censor the impression you give to other women?

When facing financial struggles as a couple, be sure to make time

to listen and talk to one another. Remember that there is not one right way.

Your task is to find a solution that feels right enough to you both.

CHAPTER 7

....

Love

I wish we had talked about money more. We came from completely different backgrounds. The few times I actually talked about growing up poor, I had to get drunk in order to tell him about it. —MICHELLE

LOVE IS AN ELEMENTAL FEELING. We all need to be loved—it's a basic need that we have from the moment of birth. Babies die without love and caring. For many of us, love is what ultimately makes life worthwhile. Love is also one of the measures by which we understand and interpret others' behavior.

Money is a powerful currency for both expressing and withholding love. In our culture, money is one of the prime ways we take care of others and are taken care of ourselves. Money can make our caring concrete. When someone pays for our dinner, gives us a gift, or even is willing to help support us, we see these actions as representing the love they feel toward us. We use it to express our love of ourselves. Because we use money in so many ways to intentionally convey a message of love, we often find it hard to separate money from love. So we see how we can get confused and think that money is talking about love, or its lack, when in fact it's not.

LOVE AND MONEY

Money can be used to express love, but sometimes, money is just money. And when money is just being money, but we feel it represents love from a partner, a parent, or even God, we're projecting. It's the projection of other motives and meanings onto money that causes us to react as though money were something else—the measure of our lovability in this case. For example, it felt to me that my father didn't love me very much because he didn't offer to help me financially. I felt this when we were in line together at the grocery store buying food for the dinner I was about to make for him and he wouldn't chip in to pay for the food, or when he wouldn't offer to pay for a portion of my plane ticket to visit him after he moved across the country.

It wasn't that he couldn't afford to help me out, but as I eventually found out, he didn't think that parents should help their children with money because nobody had helped him financially. If I'd realized that this was why he wasn't more generous with me, I might have felt less rejected when he didn't offer to help buy the bag of groceries or plane ticket. And I would have taken all our money dealings less personally if I had understood then, as I do now, that my father never felt he had enough money for himself, let alone enough to share. We never talked about money, and I had neither the tools nor the emotional distance to be able to see his inner relationship to money.

In my relationship with my father, money was not a trustworthy sign of his love. How people treat us with money has much more to do with them and their relation to money than it does with how they feel about us. Some people are more generous with their money than others, but not necessarily more generous with their love. Some, like my mother, use money to express love, and they give and receive gifts as if the gifts were the essence of love. Others never use money to express love.

So though some of us may quickly interpret money as a sign of love, it may not be a reliable indicator. Do I love my child more because I gave her a larger than usual check this year for her birthday? Does my not wanting to share my bonus mean I don't love my partner? Does it indicate my love for my friends if I don't pay for my friend's dinner one night but the next night I do with another friend? Does my not wanting to pay for the entire weekend away express a lack of love for my partner? Though it may be difficult for us to comprehend at times, love is not always involved with money matters.

FAMILY LOVE

From allowances to inheritances, money is often a medium through which love speaks within families. We use money to support, encourage, nourish, and nurture those we love. We use money both to provide necessities as well as to fulfill deep desires. When we're at our best, for example, the pocket money we hand our children is infused with love. And it is received with excitement and innocent expectation—from the uncle who sends us ten dollars on every birthday, to the young girl who longs to have a sibling and takes her piggy bank full of coins to her mother, saying she wants to buy a sister. Sadly, money sometimes is the *only* medium someone has for expressing their love.

Money can also be an unloving and harsh communicator in families. We use it to control, manipulate, bind, punish, enable, obligate, and infantilize those we love. We use it to compete, undermine, and express our dislike for one another. We may, for example, withhold tuition unless our daughter studies what and where we want her to, or we may give more money to one child than to another.

Much of the time, dealing with money and love is not so straightforward. There are lots of twists and turns in the correlation between money and love, as we will come to see. Sometimes, for example, giving is the unloving act—and withholding is what is most loving. And just as our feelings and behavior concerning being loved and loving can be unpredictable at times, so also can our feelings and behavior about love and money. How we behave *with* money is influenced by how we are feeling *about* money: anxious or confident, greedy or generous, stressed or relaxed, deprived or satisfied, a failure or a success, and overwhelmed or resilient. It is also influenced by our general mood, be it loving, happy, hurt, or angry. Is it any wonder that we have conflicts over money with those we love?

145

Money is a convenient vehicle for expressing our psychological needs, often in unconscious and primitive ways. Other motives can exist side by side with expressions of love. For example, we might foster an adult daughter's financial dependency out of a desire to support the career she is pursuing. Simultaneously, it provides reassurance of my value as a mother and reinforces her needing me. I might not even be aware of these latter motivations in sending her a monthly check.

So indeed, the intertwining of money and love is tricky. We need to develop our abilities to give, not give, ask for, and receive money—with the goal of being able to use the best response in whatever family situation we face. So much in the equation is dependent on the individuals involved that there is no formula for us to follow. Where love and money come together, it to pays to give the best attention we can, be in the present, and talk to one another about how we are feeling.

Questions to consider regarding family, money, and love:

- Was money used in your family growing up to express love, approval, or disapproval?
- Have you felt loved through gifts of money?
- If so, when and how?
- Was money ever used in an attempt to "buy" your love?
- If so, was it successful?
- Have you ever used money as a means of maintaining a relationship?
- Was anyone in your family given more than others were?
- Did you ever feel jealous of displays of love between other family members that involved money?
- If you are giving money to family members, how is it working out for you?
- What do you think your motivation is?
- Do you have the expectation that you will earn their love and approval?
- Out of love, do you ever give more than you can truly afford to give?

- If so, why?
- Do you give money conditionally or unconditionally?
- What are the conditions, if any?

WHEN MONEY EQUALS LOVE

One of the ways we interpret whether or not we are loved, first as children and then as adults, is by what we are given and not given, both emotionally and materially. Money can be taken as a reassurance that we are loved or an indication that we are not.

Jenny described about one such, seemingly inconsequential, disappointment in her life:

> I fell in love with a harmonica when I was about five years old. We went to the music store fairly often, and every time I'd stare at the harmonicas in the case. I continually asked my parents to get this particular one for me. After about six months, they gave that very harmonica to my brother for his birthday and told me I was too young to have it. I was crushed and took it to mean that they loved my brother more than me.

We confuse the giving of money and things as love—it's hard not to. We each have countless stories of money and things not given. If the slights, punishments, or acts of neglect we experience are part of a repeated pattern, we develop an interpretation, a belief, about why this is happening to us—perhaps we believe our partner doesn't love us or our parents don't love us, or love us less than the sibling who got the harmonica. Or we might decide we are undeserving of whatever we long for, including their love.

Questions to ponder about the relationship between love and money:

- Do you correlate the money you are given with love?
- Have you ever used money to test whether you are loved? Please describe.

GIVING LOVE THROUGH MONEY

Giving and receiving money can bring intense pleasure as well as strengthen the love between family members. It is an expression of an elemental wish to be of help, a desire that arises from caring. As women, we are often concerned for the happiness and needs of others, and we give whenever we are able. Most of us know the feeling of gratification that comes from giving, either to celebrate an occasion, to help someone in need, or to share what we have.

Giving money can be beneficial, benefiting both the recipient and the giver—though sometimes, it may not feel 100 percent good. Linda described how challenging it was after her husband lost his job and she was the sole provider:

> *Those two years took a toll on me. Money worries are one of the most stressful things. We still lived better than most people in the world do, but you compare yourself to how you used to live. I've always worked full time and when we both were working, we didn't live extravagantly. But I had a horse—horses are money pits—and we traveled. It was very hard to sell my horse and to not take any time off. I had to pick up extra work. We'd always kept our money separate, and now I had to make my income and savings work for both of us. I grew up spoiled, and so it wasn't a pretty side of me when I couldn't be my spoiled self anymore.*
>
> *In order to support my husband, whom I loved very dearly, I needed to look at my dream of how I thought my life should be and question my expectations. We learned that having money worries didn't make us different people or love each other any less at the end of the day. We discovered that we can get through bad times, including my anger and my husband's depression. And we're stronger now as a couple. Some of our new strength came out of my being able to support us financially for those two years, and his being able to receive the support.*

Giving money can also be detrimental, even when we give out of love. We can give in ways that are hurtful, financially as well as emotionally, to ourselves and others. Sometimes the sacrifices we make are too large. We can be overly possessive—using money to control and keep our children and others tied to us. We can be overprotective—using money to keep our children and others from struggling with hardships and decisions that could bring them experiences and learning.

Rose gave money to her son every time he asked for almost forty years. After she developed dementia, though she might not recognize her grandchildren or friends, the minute she saw her son she went to look for her checkbook. Even through the fog of her dementia, she remembered his need for money and her need to give it to him. Rose actually ended up having enough money to live out her life, but it cost her in other ways. Before her dementia, though she never stopped giving to him, she was angry that her son contacted her only when he needed money. Additionally, Rose's giving so much attention to her son, always worrying about him and giving him money, made her daughter feel less loved in comparison. This was hurtful to her daughter, and though she remained devoted to Rose, over the years it took its toll on her love for her mother. And when Rose died, there was little money left for the family. The son, who had become dependent on the handouts, was left high and dry.

Many mothers, my own included, cannot stop giving reflexively—sometimes even when they want to. Roberta had raised her daughter as a single mother, and when her own daughter had children, Roberta wanted to help so her grandkids wouldn't go without. A pattern was established of giving her daughter money—not only cash but also car insurance, cell phone coverage, and so on. This went on for sixteen years. Roberta told the Emotional Currency group, "I thought it was just a phenomenon in the black community, but I spoke to a white lawyer who's supporting her daughter. And it's not just women; there's a Bank of Daddy as well."

Many mothers have difficulty saying no. But Roberta was eventually able to:

I closed the Bank of Mama. It wasn't easy, but it was necessary. Money was wreaking havoc on our relationship; it was so unhealthy. I realized that I wasn't going to have enough to take care of myself when I got older. I'd been harping on her to get her own insurance and phone, but she never did it. When I closed the Bank of Mama, she took care of business.

*The first several months afterward things were very testy. But my daughter is
not only taking care of business, she's checking in with me more, and there's a new
freedom between us. With money involved, there were certain things I had to know,
things I didn't want to know.*

Roberta had to separate money from love in order to do what was
best for both her and her daughter, and, therefore, the most loving thing
she could do. Luckily it brought them closer, but there was no guarantee
it would turn out that way.

Increasingly, adult children are being called on to help their parents
financially. This can feel like an opportunity to lovingly return the
care they received from the parents growing up. Sammie sends her
elderly mother a monthly check, which gives her mother enough extra
income to turn the heat on when she gets cold without worry about
the fuel bill or to go out to eat occasionally when she might otherwise
skip a meal. These checks give Sammie a chance to directly express
her love for her mother and give her mother an opportunity to feel
well-loved. Sammie feels fortunate to have the means to express her
love in this way.

Ask yourself:

- How do you use money to express your love through taking
  care of others?

WITHHOLDING LOVE

Sometimes parents use money to withhold love or to give the message
that a child doesn't deserve their love. Susan's mother repeatedly told her
that she was bad and unlovable. The message was passively reinforced
by her father, who never intervened on his daughter's behalf. Susan
believed what her mother said and carried this belief about herself well
into her adulthood:

My mother projected all the bad onto me. Anything that disturbed her was due to the way I was or my fault. And she projected all the good onto my sister. When I was in the sixth grade, totally out of the blue, our parents told us we could no longer attend the private school we had always gone to and dearly loved. They said it was because I was too proud and thought that I was better than the other kids; going to the public school would teach me to come off my high horse. And years later, early in my freshman year in college, my mother found out that I had tried alcohol and sent me a letter stating that their financial support was over. That was thirty years ago, and my parents haven't given me one dime since. I put myself through college and a master's degree.

For years, Susan used money to punish herself and reinforce her sense of being unlovable:

I always had enough money to provide for my food and shelter, but I never saved anything. When I had extra, I gave it away, to ensure that I was always just on the edge with money. I think this was a form of perpetuating my mother's punishment of me. It was a reliable way to always feel bad about myself.

Susan worked hard emotionally to understand that the bad wasn't actually in her, but was rather the result of her mother's projections. She developed a love for herself and, in so doing, came to feel that she was lovable. When she was far along in her healing, she initiated a conversation with her father; what he told her helped her to root out any lingering feelings of badness within her:

I asked him about the tuition decisions and he confessed that, really, he hadn't been able to continue to afford either tuition, at the private grammar school or the university. I asked him why he hadn't just told me this at the time, and he said that he hadn't been able to admit that there wasn't enough money. His whole identity is as a caretaker, so he couldn't bear it that he couldn't help. I cried with unimaginable relief when he told me that he loved me and that I was never a bad person, that I was always a good girl. I realized that he just couldn't stand up to my mother.

HAVING OUR FEELINGS HURT—
THROUGH MONEY

Because we don't usually talk about money matters, we lack the vocabulary and the knowledge about how to respond to financial exchanges that have been hurtful to us. A family or couple in which the members can speak to one another about being hurt by an exchange having to do with money is exceedingly rare, and hurt feelings often go underground.

It's commonly understood that being disinherited or cut out of a will can be extremely wounding. But I don't think it's common knowledge that small financial inequalities and slights can be the cause of long-term hurts as well. Miscommunications can happen easily, but they may not even be recognized, let alone repaired between those involved. A sister gives her elderly mother a monthly check to help with her expenses, thinking that her other siblings are doing the same, but they are not. When she discovers this, she resents that she is the only one helping. But she says nothing of this to them. Her siblings, it turns out, thought it was just an idea that had been discussed but hadn't been agreed to. Or in a slightly different scenario, another set of siblings all agree to help their mother, but one brother stops sending his contribution after just a few months. Their mother, with much hesitation, finally tells one of her daughters about this. It's not the first time he hasn't paid his way, even though, of all of the siblings he makes the most money. It is the rare family in which issues and feelings such as these can be brought up, or worked through, even though they may well impact, to some degree, the feelings of love felt among the siblings.

Couples are fertile ground for emotional hurt involving money. Feelings of jealousy arise from our partner or spouse being more generous with others than they are with us, perhaps taking their best friend out to dinner regularly to nicer restaurants than they go to with us. Or they make decisions involving spending or investing money without consulting us. Or they may complain about how wasteful we are for buying too much food, when they find the apples rotting in the refrigerator, but don't bill their clients for the money they are owed.

If the hurt involving money is big enough or repeated often enough, we will need to address the situation with the other person or people involved. As with all interpersonal relations, it is often a matter of sharing our feelings and clarifying what took place. Bringing such situations to light helps the misunderstanding and hurt to go away. Other times the incident is evidence of a deeper pattern of disrespect or selfishness and is more difficult to resolve. Paying attention to our hurt feelings is a way to uncover that which needs to be healed within ourselves and within our relationship with a significant other and family members.

Questions to consider regarding hurt feelings:

- Can you think of ways that you've been hurt in money exchanges?
- How did the other person hurt you?
- Can you imagine talking about your feelings with that person?
- Are there ways you have been hurtful to others in dealing with money?

COUPLES, LOVE, AND MONEY

Money can be a powerful attractor—even an aphrodisiac. And even though we all know that money can't buy love, some of us act as though it could. Clearly, many women (and men) consider their financial resources in choosing a partner—for some it is a deal breaker. Some women need their partners, whether male or female, to be industrious, generous, and either have financial resources or have the potential to make money. For others, regardless of their own financial situation, it matters very little. And, of course, there are the concerns of ones' parents, which may or may not hold influence. A client of mine said that her father's response when she told him who she wanted to marry was to say, "But he doesn't have any money, does he? You should think hard about this decision. I know a very nice, young man you could marry who has already saved $50,000."

As the gender roles rapidly shift among couples (whether hetero-sexual or same sex), some of the traditional ways money expresses love are changing. Men are no longer necessarily sole earners who show their love by providing for their family, and women are no longer expected to make them feel loved by being financially dependent on them. But there are still lots of other ways that money is used to express love, or its absence, in couples.

Money is one of the biggest sources of stress and arguments. Dis-parities in values, income, and spending styles create challenges for all couples, along with familial differences in how money was handled. All sorts of power issues play out with money. And money issues exac-erbate underlying problems in relationships. Though money problems are often listed as the number one reason for divorce, or at least in the top ten reasons couples split up, it's actually not money in itself that causes relationships to end. It's actually—here I go again—what money represents that causes the unresolvable conflicts. The couple needs to work at—the level of what money symbolizes emotionally—to move through money impasses. The only way to determine the nature and origins of these difficulties is communication: both partners must be willing and able to look at their emotions and to understand their own as well as their partner's relationship to money. Sometimes this requires professional help. Fran and Tom are such a couple.

Fran had been financially self-sufficient before she married Tom. They both worked and they kept their money separate except for a joint checking account for shared expenses. Tom contributed more to the account based on his higher salary. They loved each other and their life together, but when they came to see me in the fourth year of their mar-riage, they were close to divorce over Fran's credit card debt.

After they had been married a very short time, Fran began ask-ing Tom for short-term loans to pay off her monthly credit card bill rather than incur interest charges. Although she had not previously overspent her earnings, now she was. Tom had savings that he could easily access, and she always paid him back within a few months, but Tom was uncomfortable with Fran's chronic overspending and insisted she stop. Although she always agreed that she would, she toned down her spending only long enough to repay him and then began running up debt again. After this happened repeatedly, Tom felt he could no longer trust Fran to keep her word.

As we explored why this was so distressing to Tom, he described how his father had constantly exaggerated how much money he spent, made, and had. For example, his father would say that he had spent hundreds of dollars on a birthday bike for his son, but Tom knew that it was actually a $49.95 model. He wasn't sure why his father had acted that way, but in response, Tom had consciously chosen to be very honest and responsible about money in his own life. More than the overspending, it was Fran's lack of integrity in her money dealings that was causing Tom to want to flee the relationship.

Meanwhile, Fran was frustrated with her new and perplexing over-spending; she needed to uncover its elusive source within herself. She had taken pride in being an independent woman. Through our work together, Fran came to realize that getting married in her midthir-ties had confused her psychological boundaries in unanticipated ways. She had always been so invested in being self-sufficient, emotionally as well as financially, that she didn't have a repertoire of ways to be needy. Running up debt and asking for money, she discovered, was an uncon-scious way to show that she needed him. Being in debt provided her worth a direct experience and expression of her needing Tom. Embar-rassed as she was to admit this, she and Tom could then discuss other ways he could take care of her. Tom let her know he wanted to take care of her, just not monetarily.

As we've just seen, unmet needs in couples can be indirectly expressed through money. Sometimes, as in the following story, one partner has difficulty with the other having any needs at all. Michelle was one of five siblings growing up in a family with few financial resources. After paying her own way through college, Michelle went to work in a lucra-tive career. After a few years, however, it felt empty to her and she left it to do work she was passionate about, which paid her far less money.

Though she hadn't married Sean for his money, Michelle was attracted to the security that his paycheck and his parents' resources brought to their life together. And though it was unconscious at the time, she sees now that she had hoped that being with him would make her life easier financially. From the beginning of their relationship, she ignored signs that Sean had difficulty sharing. For instance, they split all their expenses exactly down the middle, even though he had far more resources from his income and family's money.

Being around his wealthier lifestyle gave her a taste for nicer clothes and eating in more expensive restaurants, the cost of which she put on her credit card. And while he thought nothing of indulging himself with nice clothes and expensive tickets to sports events, he never offered to pay for any of the things she wanted or to take them to places they went. She grew resentful and angry about how little he helped her out or shared with her. Though conflicted about leaving after six years of marriage, she felt so unloved and disheartened that she moved out.

Soon after, she came to an Emotional Currency Workshop, where she expressed her regret:

> I wish we had talked about money more. We came from completely different backgrounds. Our money talks always focused on his wanting me to earn more. The few times I actually talked about growing up poor, I had to get drunk in order to tell him about it. His growing up with wealth, as well as his having more money than I did, activated my shame about growing up with nothing. He was judgmental about my family, and I felt protective about them. So I stopped talking about them with him.

Although Michelle felt capable of taking care of herself, and didn't think she had needed Sean to take care of her in order to feel loved, she experienced that he was withholding his love through his stinginess. As a result, she continually felt needy and humiliated. Michelle offered to leave the marriage with no alimony because she couldn't bear to ask for anything from him.

Michelle's reluctance to examine fully and talk about her money emotions caused her to stifle her own needs. It also left her with doubt about the cause of her ex's withholding behavior. She'll never really know. I can guess that he was narcissist in ways that prevented him from seeing or caring about her needs. Perhaps he was spoiled by his parents and felt so entitled to being taken care of that he didn't understand the kinds of caretaking required by both people, in order for a relationship to thrive. Or it could have been that he needed her to make a larger amount of money as a kind of test to make sure that she wasn't after him for his money. Perhaps their struggles had other socioeconomic class origins as well, or ethnic or cultural differences that contributed to their impasse. It could have been some or all of these reasons plus others that would have been revealed through sharing their emotional reactions to money. Michelle's regret is potent, because she will never know if their difficulties could have been worked through if they could have talked about money. Michelle's story is also more evidence of the powerful taboo against talking about money, even in couples.

Money challenges do not only affect heterosexual relationships. They can also cause deep hurt—or encourage deeper intimacy—in homosexual relationships as well. However, women in same-sex couples often have added social, cultural, and financial pressures that arise from the lack of legal recognition of their relationships and from homophobia.

And though many lesbian couples suffer from the lower earning capacity of a two-woman couple, Ella and Betty's issues arose from *having* money. Ella had always had a lot of money and Betty grew up solidly middle class. Though they brought vastly different financial resources to their relationship, they were able to forge a true financial and emotional partnership, within the legal limitations that lesbian and gay couples face. They described some of the steps they took in the process. Ella started her money memoir:

> *Early in our being together, I wanted Betty's salary to go for her own bills and for me to pay for everything else, including the house, entertainment, food, travel, and going to restaurants. But it turned out that I wasn't entirely comfortable paying for everything—it took some getting used to. I confess that if I were a man that it would have been easier for me to do. It was difficult, too, because I'd grown up being told I shouldn't tell a man how much money I had, because they'd want to marry me for money. And that I shouldn't share my wealth with a person, only with society. So we had to work on all the emotional issues of being together that were tied to money, some of them having to do with being a same-sex couple.*

Money highlighted, as it can for many couples, the issues that came up for each of them as they grew closer. Betty described some of her issues:

I had just gotten out of a fifteen-year marriage where I'd been a model of financial responsibility. But I went crazy when we divorced. And then it freaked me out that I'd fallen in love with a woman. I wasn't to be trusted with my own money, let alone Ella's. It was a rocky beginning, but little by little things stabilized and we made headway. After a few years, it became clear to us that Ella hated to take care of her money and that I was actually good at it. So I took responsibility for it, though not control over it.

For me, having money has never been that important. I didn't want to not have money, but beyond that I didn't really care. I chose my career based on what I wanted to do, not on how much money I would earn. And when I divorced, the divorce lawyer made me sign an agreement that I wouldn't sue him, wouldn't sue the divorce lawyer, because I just walked away from the marriage when I could have gotten a financial settlement. But I didn't want money from my ex.

Betty was able to help Ella make peace with having wealth and begin to enjoy using it. Ella recounted in her money memoir:

As our love deepened we decided to become a family. Our journey to have a child strengthened our trust of one another. And it became clear how much we completed one another. So it started to feel to me that it was an utter insult that I was pinching pennies with Betty. I'd hit some kind of emotional wall and say, "I'm not going to pay." I was wildly scared of being taken advantage of. But watching so closely what she was spending came to feel terrible to me. She had stopped working when the baby came, and she made all our lives function so beautifully. We had plenty of money. In addition to my inheritance, I was paid extraordinarily well for the work I did in the world. So I had to rethink my being overly frugal.

I'd spent my whole life being "cheap." We had wealth growing up, but we never had any help, we didn't belong to a country club. I didn't have a car in high school— my parents made me ride my bike to school. My parents had good solid values. I was selectively cheap, so I could pay for an expensive meal only to balk at having to pay for valet parking. So I'd always rebelled against my money. Creativity was my worth, not my money. Betty helped me to become comfortable having money and using it. We had become a real partnership and I wanted our money lives to reflect that—I shared my money with her."

Getting married was an important psychological ritual for Ella and Betty, but it didn't bring the legal protections and benefits that heterosexual couples enjoy. They have spent much time, effort, and money trying to gain some degree of economic protection for Betty, should Ella die first. Even with consultations with knowledgeable, creative, and expensive lawyers, they have nowhere near what legally married couples have.

Ask yourself:

- If you are in a relationship, how does money inhibit, enhance, or express love?
- If you are in a same-sex relationship, what are the issues that are specific to lesbian couples regarding money and love that you experience?

DIVORCE AND MONEY

When the conflict in a romantic relationship is deep and damaging enough that a couple divorces or separates, there can be bitter battles over money and property that result in fallout long after financial matters are resolved. With separations of long-term same-sex partners there are not legally binding laws for the separation of assets, which can make for difficult discussions about what is most "fair." As in the case of legal divorce, feelings of disappointment, rejection, betrayal, hurt, and anger intertwine with money discussions. The legal system is designed to reduce money and financial issues to concrete and quantifiable formulas. But even though there is no place in the legal system for the emotional or symbolic aspects of money, they are omnipresent.

Money can be used to fend off or fan the flames of feelings of loss and fear of the unknown. It is common for a sense of financial entitlement to arise out of an experience of feeling betrayed. It is also not uncommon for a partner to walk away, without taking what they are entitled to, out of feeling they can't win the fight, are tired of fighting, or feel guilty for not keeping his or her partner happy or the marriage intact.

If there are children, the fights can go on indefinitely over child support and payment of child expenses. Sometimes, as in Elena's case, parents directly involve their children:

> *Both my parents were like adolescents emotionally and not able to see me as the little girl I was. Instead, they used me as a messenger about money. My mother would complain to me, "We don't have enough money." And my father would ask me, "Why isn't she managing her money better?" And just as he was about to drop me off at my mother's house, he would throw lots of figures at me that I was supposed to convey to my mother. It was confusing and I'd be swimming with emotions.*

Elena was helplessly stuck in the role of the communicator between her warring parents. Though these memories are still painful to her, through much inner work she forged her own relationship to money, which was not at all like that of either parent, and freed herself from being caught in the middle.

Questions about divorce:

- Has a divorce, either your own or that of your parents, impacted your feelings about money?
- Describe the money circumstances of the divorce in some detail and the effects of the divorce on your relationship with money.
- Has a termination of your long-term relationship impacted your relationship with money?
- If so, describe.
- If you are partnered with someone who has divorced or separated from a long-term relationship where there were money issues, either during the relationship or in its dissolution, how does that impact your partner and how he or she deals with you involving money?
- What are your feelings about the situation?

FINAL ACTS: WILLS

When people die, their wills are a final expression of how they felt about others in their lives. What's included in a will can have a beneficial effect, or it can be hurtful and damaging in both intentional and in unintentional ways.

My Aunt Jo's will taught me a lot about money and the power of wills. We had been almost like mother and daughter at times and very close, particularly during a period when my parents had been preoccupied with my sister's problems. However, my aunt had so strongly disapproved of several choices I had made, especially the university I went to, that we became estranged for a while. Our relationship warmed over the years, and by the time of her death, we had become close again—though cautiously so. Despite that, she left all of her considerable estate to one of my half-brothers, whom I'll call Mark, excluding completely my other brother, whom I'll call Charlie, and me.

Although it made some sense to me that I could have been left out, what perplexed me was Aunt Jo cutting out Charlie and his family. She was always bragging about Charlie—"my nephew the judge"—plus he had two children who would need to go to college, and my aunt highly valued education. So why was he excluded as well? Her decision also confused me because Mark had made enough money in business that he retired at a young age to play drums in a band. Mark lived frugally, didn't have a family, and even he would have said that he had absolutely no need for any additional money. So why did she give it all to Mark? I finally came up with an explanation that satisfied me, though, of course, I will never know if my explanation accurately portrayed my aunt's intentions.

I had always known Aunt Jo was jealous of my mother's beauty, her attractiveness to men, and her natural warmth. But I thought that this jealousy had been balanced by Aunt Jo being more intelligent, sophisticated, and well-traveled. I also imagined that her jealousy was somewhat softened by the emotional pains my mother suffered in her life. Aunt Jo had no children, and she had tried hard to win affection from me and my brothers. As an adult Mark was not close to my mother and was in fact at times closer to Aunt Jo. At the time I thought he was being rewarded for bringing more love into her life. But as I put two and two together, I saw how naïve my thinking had been. I realized that he had been rewarded in her will for *not* being close to our mother. And that Charlie and I had been punished for *not* betraying our mother.

But the will had felt more destructive to me than mere punishment. I came to realize that it revealed how deeply envious she was of my mother, including the close relationships Charlie and I each had with her. I felt the knife of Aunt Jo's envy, trying to hurt my mother through me. I also couldn't help wonder if she intended to cause ill will between Mark, Charlie, and me.

Once I made emotional sense of her will, at least in my own heart and mind, it didn't bother me. In fact being left out of her will became a badge of pride and a validation of my love for my mother. I was proud that I hadn't let myself be controlled and manipulated by my aunt in hope of inheriting her money.

On the other side of the family, I experienced the generosity and inclusiveness of my Aunt Evelyn and my Uncle Dan. They also had no children and left everything they owned in equal gifts to their five siblings and four nieces. I was touched by their statement of equal love for all of their family members.

In no way do I mean to imply there is less love in families where there is no money to bequeath. Rather, that when there *is* money, who inherits, how equitably, and under what conditions all send powerful messages about the heart of the person who died and how they felt about the living.

Some of the most emotionally traumatic money stories involve convoluted inheritances. One such story is of Wendy, whose father died suddenly when she was fourteen and she inherited almost all of his estate. Only a small share went to her mother, and her half sister from her mother's first marriage received nothing. It wasn't a total surprise that her father would leave such a will because he and Wendy's mother constantly and openly fought about which of the daughters they would each leave their money to. Her father clearly wanted to make a powerful statement about his feelings, but I have to wonder if he really intended it to have the impact that it did.

Wendy's inheritance drove a wedge between her and the only person she felt really close to, her half sister. Despite their closeness, they couldn't get past the hurt caused by the will. It magnified the favoritism her father had always shown Wendy, his biological daughter. And it caused Wendy to feel guilty from that day on for having been favored at the expense of her half sister. Even though, of course, Wendy's receipt of the inheritance had been her father's decision, both Wendy's mother and halfsister took out their anger on Wendy. Her mother went so far as to sue the estate for what she felt she was entitled to. We could say that Wendy's inheritance cost her more than it was worth.

Questions regarding inheritance:

- Have you received an inheritance?
- If so, what were your feelings about it?
- Do you feel jealous or envious of what someone else has inherited?
- Were you ever disinherited or treated unequally in a will?
- Have there been unequal or unfair distributions of money in you family, either recently or in the past?

PHILANTHROPY

Philanthropy comes from the heart. At its best, it is an expression of loving support for humankind and the natural world. We may give out of love for specific people or ideas. We may give out of an emotional attachment to a cause or institution. We may give for the advancement of education or science or medicine or the arts or political parties. In the United States, half of all philanthropic donations are made to religious institutions. We also may use charitable gifts of money to buy prestige, power, business and social connections, and tax write-offs.

What is distinctive to women and philanthropic giving? Women give away a larger percentage of their wealth and their incomes than do men. (We give 3.5 percent of our wealth to men's 1.8 percent.) Our growing visibility in philanthropy will increase as we are projected to inherit 70 percent of the transfer of intergenerational wealth anticipated during the next forty years. Moreover, as women have more and more money to give (in part because our husbands die before us) and as we have donated more, we have influenced how philanthropic dollars are given. As we saw with Marion Weber's creation of Funding Circles, women like to give beyond distributing dollars, in a more hands-on approach. And we like to fund projects for women and girls.

When we think of philanthropy, we often think of wealthy people making large charitable donations. Most charitable gifts, however, come in the form of smaller donations from people who do not have extraordinary means. Little gifts add up. You may not be able to give what seems like very much on an annual basis, but if you think about what you are able to give over ten, twenty, or thirty years, the amount might seem much more generous.

A woman I know who had suffered from polio as a child went door-to-door raising money for polio research while still a young girl. She observed that it was the poorer families who were not only the kindest and least suspicious of her, but also the ones that made the largest donations. Of course, there are many illustrations of the kindness and generosity of those with wealth, but that the poor—perhaps more in touch with suffering and vulnerability—give away a larger percentage of their income than do the wealthy.

Tracy Gary is a philanthropist, nonprofit entrepreneur, and the author of *Inspired Legacies: Your Step-by-Step Guide to Creating a Giving Plan and Leaving a Legacy*. In our correspondence, she observed that philanthropy focused on giving to women has the most impact:

> *Women have long been recognized as the tenders of our families and as the sources of wisdom for the greater good. Given the success of micro-lending, women's advancements, and plenty of evidence-based research, investing in women and the nonprofits they develop is seen as the investment of choice by many who seek to improve communities and the world. There are now more than 165 women's foundations worldwide and their success has taught us that when a woman is secure, her family is secure. And when that family and others are secure, a community, and then a nation can be secure. Women participating as investors and as leading donors have shifted women's position in society.*

There is perhaps no greater gift than to be a giver. Between 1972 and 1985, I gave away over $1 million, or 100 percent of an inheritance that I received, by putting it back into nonprofits that were building a better world. This came not as some act of discomfort with money and its complexities, but as an enlightened source for healing. If someone had told me that giving away money and giving of myself as a volunteer and leader would have given me such a great sense of abundance and security, I would have said, "How could that possibly be?" But so it has been. For what I have gained has been the greatest of gifts, community and sense of purpose and accomplishment.

The healing that Tracy Gary referred to is available to all of us, no matter what our means. The act of giving makes us more human by connecting us with our shared and common humanity. Additionally, it provides a sense of engagement and involvement with the world, whether we are donating simply money or our time as well. Philanthropy can also be a tool for healing conflicted feelings we may have from the origins of our money, either inherited or earned, that we feel was ill-gotten by our forebears or ourselves, or that we feel was undeserved.

Sarah Hobson, the Executive Director of New Field Foundation, ties giving money to investing in the donor's vision for the world.

Through philanthropy, we can help shape the world to be a better place—a world, for example, where priority is given to peace, where the rape of women is not a weapon of war, where women do not die unnecessarily in childbirth. As women with money to give away—at whatever level—we can use our resources for the greater good. The art is how to do so without dominating those we seek to support, and how to know how our money can make a difference. We have tremendous opportunity to link up with dynamic women's organizations all over the world that are working to solve their problems locally. Our collaboration is the way of the future.

Philanthropy can be motivated by a desire to see ourselves, and have others see us, as caring individuals. But as we use the "muscle" of giving, we can develop the need within us to give and share out of our concern and caring for others. Generosity is thought by many religions to be an essential human behavior for a spiritual life. To begin to experience generosity, try this simple Buddhist practice: pass something from your right hand to your left—feeling yourself both let go and receive. And then, as you become comfortable with this simple act of giving, extend your reach farther out into the world.

Questions to consider about giving away money:

- If you make charitable donations, what inspires you to do so?
- If you do not make charitable donations, why don't you?
- Did your family make charitable donations?
- If so, to whom and in what ways?
- Have you or your family benefited from charitable gifts, either given directly to you or to an organization or institution, that impacted your life?
- How do you decide whether to give money, how much to give, and what to give to?
- How does your decision-making process feel to you?
- Have you thought of philanthropy or an expression of love?
- If not, does that change how you might approach giving money away?

transforming your relationship with money

If you aren't living within your means,

consider why you would want to and

how you can move toward doing so.

CHAPTER 8

....

Healing Your
Relationship to Money

*My explorations on deprivation led me to deeply question my belief that I was des-
tined to go without the things that really mattered to me in life. It led me to accept
my own need, longing, and vulnerability. I connected with a new kind of security
that came from investing in my own life.* —KATE

H EALING IS AN ONGOING PROCESS IN OUR EMOTIONAL LIVES. You
may associate healing with going to the doctor or taking medicine, but healing can also describe a process of returning to emotional
health. What emotional health looks like will vary for each of us, but it
is a general sense of well-being. It involves an ability to deal with, cope
with, and adjust to life's stressors and changes. It also includes some
capacity for self-esteem, and engagement with life, as well as finding
meaning and purpose. It's not a cheerleader picture of mental health. It
may well include episodes and periods of despair, fear, anger, conflict,
and sadness. Rather, it's the resiliency to find our way through those
episodes, however long they may last, and to return to equilibrium
and well-being.

We need to make meaning out of our troublesome experiences
with money, gaining perspective through understanding what has

happened in a way that includes our feelings, and finding new ways to move forward to the future. It doesn't mean you have to give up all your quirky money behavior. You get to be a little "crazy" when it comes to money—after all, we all are. Rather, the task is to heal the parts of your relationship to money that are causing problems in your life, be it emotional or financial distress. Healing will help you to be more present, to be able to see and deal with "what is" monetarily rather than "what was" or what you wish were true. The more we are really living in the present, with awareness of our life as it is now, the healthier we can be emotionally and physically, as well as financially.

WHY DO WE NEED HEALING?

Why do we need to heal? If we don't heal the confused, conflicted, and painful emotions and beliefs we have about money in our past, they will dominate our money lives. Whether consciously or not, we relive our unexamined emotions and beliefs over and over. Examining and healing them not only makes for less emotional angst and drama, it also helps us define who we are and what we value in terms of our money life, and our life as a whole.

Clearly, not all of our feelings about past experiences with money need to be healed. Some of our money history supports and enriches our lives. Some of our money behavior doesn't present problems, even though it may appear peculiarly superstitious, penny pinching, or spendthrift. But the behavior and feelings that obstruct and interfere with how we deal with money need our attention. Repetitive problematic behavior is probably an indication of conflicting emotions and unmet needs, and can be healed once we get to the root of what is bothering us.

We cling to old destructive emotional patterns for several reasons. First, they are generally so familiar to us that they are nearly invisible, and thereby have become our reality. They offer us a predictable means of organizing our lives, no matter how distorted they may be. They provide a place of refuge from the unknown and uncertain future. Even if they are disturbing and painful, they feel safer than what is unseen and unknown. And we still often believe that these patterns protect us from our anxieties, fears, and pain.

For example, let's take another look at my attachment to the feeling of deprivation. I had lots of emotional evidence to support the belief that I would never have what I wanted in my life, including what I desired financially. Though it was often a source of sorrow and grief, I chose a feeling of deprivation over the risky and scary feelings of longing and hope. I didn't really invest much of myself in my achievements, and so none of them ever really counted to me. For instance, though I went to college and graduate school, I never did so with much interest or passion about what I was studying. I chose to just go through the motions of education, though not consciously, to avoid challenging my belief that I wasn't smart. And when I started my private practice, I satisfied myself with working part-time rather than pushing myself to be more successful. I eventually became very frustrated living a life where I protected myself too much and consequently couldn't make things happen that I really cared about. Determined to be happier, I did the inner work of questioning and challenging some of my long-held fears and self-doubts, and I stopped letting them determine what I did and how I did it. I became able, little by little, to invest more of myself in my own life.

Pain, and only pain, brings us to change our ways and heal ourselves. I've just described that it was the pain and frustration from my not living a vital and engaged life that caused me to turn inward and uncover what was in the way of my being happier. Frustration, despair, angst, anxiety, hurt, grief, unhappiness, envy, jealousy, and all the other painful emotions are catalysts of change in our lives. They motivate us to do things differently, to change our status quo.

And in fact, most of our biggest gifts come in the form of these pains, stemming from the dilemmas and struggles we face. But we don't get the "gift" part of the pain we face unless we heal it. Emotional healing demands that we stretch and grow to deal with the trouble we have, finding inner resources and outer support to help us through. That's what brings the gift, growing our selves and our souls in order to make it through. Even when we are terrified, we can gradually find a place to open our hearts where we can discover healing within us.

Many hard dilemmas present themselves to us in life, directing us to do the inner work that will help us to heal. Years after the death of my sister, my beloved stepdaughter, Anna, died. There were many times that I didn't think I could survive that loss, when I couldn't imagine ever getting out of bed or caring about the world again. I thought truly I was a marked woman to have lost two of my most beloved people, my daughter and my sister. I healed those losses, and though I weep as I write about Anna's death, now twenty years past, my heart is filled with her and with the life that I am living now. Anna's death was the biggest loss I have experienced, and it also gave me profound gifts. Experiencing her death cracked open my heart not only to more pain, but also to more appreciation of life.

You may wonder what this has to do with healing your pain about money. What I'm saying is that I know both loss and healing intimately. I have worked with countless women who have healed extraordinary losses, including emotional losses involving money. As you may know well from your own suffering, difficult experiences make us discover inner depths and resources we did not know we had—and that, no matter how dire the situation or how brutal the experience, healing can happen.

STEPS FOR HEALING

How do we heal? Here are six steps to help you heal your relationship with money.

1. Identify your troublesome emotional reaction or behavior.
2. Discover what contributes to your feeling, behaving, and thinking the way you do.
3. Explore your emotions around your troublesome reaction or behavior.
4. Be open.
5. Create a support system.
6. Accept what has been and what is.

Now let's take a closer look at each step.

Step 1: Identify your troublesome emotional reaction or behavior.

The first step in any psychological healing process, including financial, is to identify the troublesome emotional reaction or behavior. You've probably already come up with many of your own as you've read through this book—parts of yourself that are emotionally deadened, chaotic, or causing you trouble. In my case, it was an emotional issue, deprivation, which I identified. But it could also have been specific behaviors, such as not promoting my private practice, disorderly financial records, or inattention to my spending.

Step 2: Discover what contributes to your feeling, behaving, and thinking the way you do.

Once you have identified the issue or behavior, the second step toward healing is to "unpack" it by seeing what contributes to feeling, behaving, and thinking the way you do. Put your attention to it by writing, talking, thinking, or imagining about it. Try to discover how you learned to be this way, what you were taught, what you observed, and what decisions you made. Include your own subjective perspective and the bigger context, that is, what was occurring at the time in your family or in the world. See how far back in time your problem originated, perhaps even to prior generations. Looking back on our experiences gives us a different perspective from what we had at the time they occurred.

For example, my feelings of deprivation and the need to protect myself from further losses, like all of our problematic beliefs, had multiple sources. The most significant ones came from my growing-up years, including the suicide of my sister and my helplessness at making her want to live; my parents' divorce; my parents' lack of involvement in my life and their never encouraging me to take on challenges or helping me to learn new things; going to school with kids who were smarter, more attractive, richer, and who got to have and do things I could only wish for.

Once I identified the sources of my problematic beliefs, I began to look at them one by one and use them to think, write, and explore further on the theme of deprivation and protection.

Step 3: Explore your emotions around your troublesome reaction or behavior.

But as helpful as getting your head around the problem can be, you must also engage the heart by exploring your emotions around your problem relating to money. This is step three of the healing process. Observe what emotions come up as you focus on the material you are exploring. When you notice a feeling ask yourself:

- Can you identify what you are feeling?
- Is it a familiar feeling to you?
- What just happened to evoke the feeling?
- How was the feeling evoked—by a memory, something in the present, or a thought about the future?

Begin to work with the feeling. One way is to keep your attention on the emotion. See if you can amplify it; turn up the volume in a sense, in order to form a more distinct impression of it. In my case, for example, I encouraged my feeling of deprivation by saying to myself:

Why is it I can't ever have what I want?
Why, when someone admires my necklace, do I have to point out the chipped bead?
Why can't I make X dollars a year?
Why did we sell the house when we did? It's worth so much more now.
Why can't I weigh 130 pounds?

In other words, I encouraged the feeling that I can't have what I want, with a twist of a sense of martyrdom. I was specific about the money, the house, the body weight, or the love I'd never have—so that I could best identify and pinpoint the feeling.

Sometimes we have difficulty knowing what it is that we are feeling, so you may need to play with this for awhile to be able to home in on identifying your more nuanced feelings. Lean into the feeling gently in order to observe what other thoughts, memories, feelings, sensations, images, or associations might be attached to it. Let yourself free associate because a memory that arises and initially seems unrelated could hold a key. Allow yourself to carefully uncover where the feeling might be coming from. Ask yourself:

- Do you know when you first began to have this experience?
- Where do you feel it in your body?
- What are the origins of this feeling?
- Do you know anyone else who feels similarly?
- How does it impact your thinking?
- What does it make you feel like doing?

Other ways to access your feelings include talking to people with whom you feel safe to explore your feelings. Try talking with them in a free-associative way that does not involve analysis or interpretation. Make art about money—collages work even for those of us who may not feel artistic. You may also want to deepen whatever other solitary pursuits support your emotional healing, such as being outdoors, walking, running, writing, meditating, or doing yoga. Allow time for reflection. Write in your money journal, with an emphasis on feeling.

In my own story of healing, my awareness of feelings of deprivation and unhappiness with the way I limited my life eventually led me to a psychotherapist who helped me see the grief that I carried inside, but could not *feel*. Slowly I grieved my losses, especially my sister's suicide. In time, I also came to feel my anger at her—anger at not being able to share my life with her—and anger at my parents for abandoning me during my sister's troubled years. Their attention was on money—my father watching like a hawk how it was spent and my mother trying to get it to give to my sister—not on me. I grieved over my parents' failure to take care of my sister, themselves, their marriage, and me. Feeling how brokenhearted I was over the loss of my sister eventually enabled me to feel my love for her again. It allowed me to heal my heart and deeply embrace my own love of life.

Step 4: Be open.

The fourth step is to be open. Being open is essential in healing, open to the gifts that come our way. Healing gifts come in the packages of words, gestures, moments, signs, or things—even money. They may involve people, animals, plants, oceans, planets—the list of the forms they may take is endless—but they always consist of events that touch our hearts and connect us to our feelings. You overhear a conversation between a mother and daughter that helps you see something about your relationship with your mother; a clerk in a store tells you about the life-threatening illness she is facing; the beauty of a flower touches your soul. The healing power of gifts is not attached to their size or their duration—small and short, and long and large can be equally powerful medicine. They are random and fleeting moments of connection and support that others may be oblivious to because of their ordinariness. But they speak potently to you, because they resonate with something deep inside.

There were so many such gifts that helped me break through my "poor me" feelings at various stages of my healing. A small and short happening that touched me was a hummingbird that came to the window where I was standing. It hovered, on the other side of the glass, right by my face for longer than I could ever have imagined. After her death, hummingbirds became a symbol to me of my stepdaughter, Anna. (Her name was Anna Costa and there is both an Anna's hummingbird and a Costa's hummingbird.) Something in being visited by this extraordinarily delicate and beautiful hummingbird, and its symbolism, healed my heart a bit more and gave me a deeper appreciation for being alive. It was the gift of a birthday party that my husband and a friend gave for me that pushed me solidly from deprivation and irrevocably into gratitude. I generally don't have birthday parties, but they insisted on doing it and took care of everything, including surprising me with two of my favorite musicians—friends of ours—playing throughout the night. And my friend surprised me with a beautiful book she'd made, full of pictures of my life. It was all such a gift of love, that I had to receive it. And in doing so, I could no longer diminish myself.

Step 5: Create a support system.

The fifth step is to develop a support system for healing your relationship to money. Knowing that you are not alone in your struggles and pain is extremely important.

Because it is very difficult to do inner emotional work completely on your own, consider developing a support system. There are many ways to do this, and no single way is right for everyone:

- Talk with trusted family and friends.
- Consult with a psychotherapist who has done his or her own inner money work and is comfortable talking about money.
- Work with a financial planner who includes working with feelings about money as part of the planning process.
- Create a money group with a few friends where you meet to talk about money challenges, dilemmas, hopes, and dreams.
- Join an online group, at www.emotionalcurrency.com or on another site, to write about money in your life and hear from other women.
- Attend 12-step programs, such as Debtors Anonymous.

Talking with trusted others is the best form of support you can get while you are working on healing your relationship to money. I say "trusted" because before you can really explore emotionally about money, you need to know that the person you are talking with is trustworthy both about money and about feelings. So the friend who was so supportive when you were getting a divorce or figuring out whether to take the new job might not be able to "be there" for you with money issues. It's fine if the person you are talking with has their own problems with money, just as long as when they talk with you, they don't judge you or tell you what to do. Their job is to listen to you and to be curious with you about what you're dealing with, not to solve problems. We all have areas in our lives where we can listen with respect and caring, keeping others' "stuff" separate from our own. And we all have other areas where we get so flooded by our own reactions that we can't really distinguish what is coming from us and what belongs to the other person, and so we can't really help support their process.

For example, if I've just heard there are going to be layoffs in my department, I don't want to talk about it with someone whose own job and money insecurities will be so activated that they won't be able to give me the room to sort out what I feel and need to do about the situation I'm facing. I also don't want to talk about it with a friend who will immediately "fix it" with solutions and who can't tolerate my being in emotional limbo while I'm finding my way through the situation I'm facing. I want to talk to someone who can respect my feelings and my process, be a good listener, and perhaps guide me with a few thoughtful questions.

Step 6: Accept what has been and what is.

The sixth step of healing is acceptance. This occurs as you discover your own meaning in the wounded and painful places in your history with money. Your deeper understanding and insight will expand your appreciation for what you've experienced and who you are. You will use your past to help inform your decisions about money, that is, they will give you much rich information about what you value in life.

There are large events involving money that can take quite awhile to accept. I've told you of the healing that I've done around my parents' money conflicts. Seeing what brought them to deal with one another in the angry and sometimes cruel ways they did, helped to take much of the sting out of those memories for me. I have come to accept, without blaming either of them, that they could not find common ground through the difficulties my sister presented our family. It is clichéd, but I think true to say, that they did the best they could. Experiencing my sister's drug addiction and my parents' endless arguments about money during my adolescence was enormously painful to me, but it destroyed neither my spirit nor my heart. And I can now see that it left me with a strong need to find my own perspective on the value of money.

TALKING ABOUT MONEY

In order to converse about money, we need to develop both our talking and listening skills. Listening without an agenda and without doing anything can be profoundly helpful in someone's healing. This is the kind of listening for which there is no need to come up with responses or solutions—they will only get in the way. Rather, it's a kind of active listening in which you respectfully attend to what the other person is saying with curiosity. It's a "being" process, not a "doing" process. Listening in this way supports the person talking in unseen ways as they explore their feelings.

Sometimes we need to tell another how we feel about something, in this case, about money, in order to heal. In this type of conversation, how the listener responds is not of as much concern to us as our need to tell them whatever it is we need to say. It's best to have this kind of talk only after you have given the topic much thought and have a very clear sense of what you are feeling and need to say. Ask that the other person listen in the style I've just described. Let them know that you will give them time to respond, if they want to, but that first you need them just to listen to what you are saying.

Sometimes discussions are part of the healing process. In these conversations you will need to actively listen as well as talk. Try to understand the other person's positions and feelings. Listen for the underlying message given to you about money. Think about the ultimate outcome you want from the conversation—if you are working toward understanding, forgiveness, or acceptance—so that you can stay focused on the healing results you desire.

TAKING YOUR EMOTIONAL MONEY PULSE

Now and then you'll want to take your emotional money "pulse" to see if the steps you are taking toward healing are helpful. Remember that behavioral change often lags behind emotional change. Know that sometimes when we feel nothing is happening, much can be taking place in the depths of our psyches. Healing happens in phases, and not all of it is conscious, obvious, or even predictable. It is an organic process. Sometimes we have to go backward before we can go forward. With each phase, there will be a new sense of freedom and vision about your relationship to money.

These suggestions for working with your money injuries are multi-layered, and obviously healing will take time. Some issues and feelings can be understood quickly, especially if you've worked with them many times before. Other feelings may take years to penetrate. There's no rush! Sometimes you can benefit from healing just a few layers. Sometimes you need to get to the root of the problem before you experience significant relief.

As you now know, healing our money lives involves not only our relationship to money, but other emotional terrain as well. I learned to use money in ways that enhanced my new feelings of being vibrantly alive rather than pinching pennies and reinforcing my old feelings of being unworthy of such an investment. The more I was able to care about the things I truly valued and to embrace those things that deeply mattered to me, the happier I was and the more I was able to generate money to support myself.

FACING THE DARKNESS, TURNING TO THE LIGHT

We must face the darkness to heal. In order to see the reality of money—good and bad, light and dark—we must also discover those aspects that fall in shadow. The shadow side of money often contains the feelings of personal pain, humiliation, self-criticism, and shame that we all have in relationship to money, but that remain largely unconscious. It includes our selfish, competitive, envious, and greedy feelings. By acknowledging and facing the shadow side of money within, we become more fully human and more fully ourselves. By facing the shadow and the darkness within us, we can also begin to turn to the light as well. As is said, out of the darkness comes the light.

When we refuse to face the shadow and the darkness, we continually repeat our broken life patterns from the past. This brokenness blinds us to the opportunities, as well as dangers, in the present. Healing is not about forgetting the past—the past is a part of who we are. It brings deep-felt experience and wisdom to our lives. Healing helps us to contain and integrate the past. As we become more whole and grounded, we see our relationship with money more clearly, which enables us to determine what information or action is necessary in a given situation. We become more trustworthy responders to the situations we face and are better able to support ourselves emotionally and financially. Healing allows us to realistically engage with the money we have, identify how we might make more money, or decide what we want to do with the money we have. We are freer to know what we want to spend, save, invest, or give away.

Ask yourself:

- What is one money behavior or area of your emotional money life that you would like to change?
- How will you approach healing it?
- What kinds of help do you need, and from whom do you need it, in order to support your healing?

If you tend to think,

"This shouldn't be happening to me,"
the best response to tell yourself is,

"But it is happening to me."

CHAPTER 9

Making Your Money
Action Plan

Money is the last thing I pay attention to. But not attending to it costs me a lot
of money. And even though I tell myself it will just work out, it really doesn't.
Now that I understand some of my fears about money, I've come up with the three
next steps I can take: I'm going to talk to my partner about sharing our household
expenses more fairly, talk to my mother about her retirement plans, and work on
healing my shame about filing for bankruptcy ten years ago. —JOANNE

T HIS IS THE SHORTEST CHAPTER OF THE BOOK, but I hope it will
be the most lasting one for you. As much as our inner lives are
important, I find them most potent when they are integrated into our
outer lives. We can get so bogged down in feelings that we never take
action. However, we can also act prematurely without considering our
emotions and how they affect our actions. Your money action plan, or
MAP, integrates your feelings and financial concerns, your heart and
your mind, into your actions, enabling you to come to the best solutions
regarding money matters.

Begin your MAP by identifying three actions you can commit to
taking over the next three months that will improve your relationship
to money. You may have come up with these next steps already. In fact,

they may have been on your to-do list for a very long time. Or it may require a bit of thought to outline what you need to do next.

You read Joanne's MAP in the epigraph to this chapter. Like Joanne's, your MAP may consist of financial actions as well as internal emotional work. Here are some other actions that graduates of Emotional Currency Workshops have committed themselves to taking:

- Interview financial planners
- Deal with tax and retirement account issues
- Consolidate credit card debt
- Write more about the history of a personal money dilemma
- Refrain from using credit cards for a specific amount of time
- Talk to a family member or friend about a specific money issue
- Form a women's group focused on money
- Talk to a friend or your boss about frustrations regarding your income or salary
- Donate money to a cause or organization
- Find a money mentor
- Attend Debtors Anonymous meetings
- Talk with parents about their estate planning

Here's what one participant wrote:

After taking your workshop, I was aware that I needed to examine my emotional relationship to money. I wasn't sure how to do this, but I used the three steps I created for my MAP to guide me: (1) Dream Big and ponder the emotions raised. (2) Discuss CD [certificate of deposit] with a financial advisor (which meant, to me, FIND a financial advisor). (3) See "what is" about my income.

I did the legwork to open myself to new ways of thinking about money. I looked at www.yourmoneyoryourlife.com, I bought a few lottery tickets in order to feel less tight with money in general and more free about spending it. I won enough to keep buying more tickets for a few weeks, but then that fizzled. I asked my yoga teacher if she would link her website to my massage website. I got a few calls that way. I also renegotiated my lease with my landlords when the recession hit to reduce my overhead. Then I started contract work with a local hospice. This saw me through some tough times and even allowed me to add to my savings. Then I found a financial advisor. About that time, my SEP-IRA was spit out of the brokerage where it had been languishing because they told me it was too small. With a few carefully chosen friends and associates, I have explored a new arrangement with a locally based firm that seems able to help me develop a reasonable financial retirement plan.

This story will continue to unfold, of course, but I feel so much more grounded with my money, and while I have a basic trust with my husband about the long-range finances in our marriage, I've become more involved in making decisions about how to manage what I earn and save and spend. I feel more generous, less stressed and vulnerable. I recently invested in our daughter's business, which is flourishing. That felt really great. I also arranged to clean up the last bits of financial involvement with another daughter, working with patience and kindness to take her off our insurance and our phone plan.

If you get stuck coming up with things to do, consider an area of your money life that needs more attention. It can be as simple as deciding to actually open your bank statement and study it every month, or it can be as involved as reassessing your finances with a financial advisor. Another way to begin is to identify one area of your money life that you'd like to change and determine what the first step would be toward making that change. It's always good to consider what help you might need in order to accomplish what you want to do and from whom you can get that help. If you want to learn more about investing, you can take a class through an educational or financial institution, you can study online, meet with a financial planner, read books, or ask your friends to teach you what they know. The next chapter lists lots of resources for gaining knowledge and getting help.

Once you have your three tasks, write them in your journal. Make a note in your calendar to assess how you've done after thirty days, and then again at the end of three months. Find a way to hold yourself accountable. That doesn't mean that you punish yourself if you haven't completed the tasks on time—it means that you work with yourself on figuring out what is in the way if you are having difficulty. You may want to share your MAP with your partner, spouse, or a friend. Perhaps meet with that person for support, either during or at the end of the three months.

Of course, this is just a beginning. After you've completed your first three steps, you can come up with another three that you commit to doing in another three-month period, and then another three, and so on. The structure is there to encourage your ongoing work with money—and given the realities of modern life, we continually have new financial concerns and tasks to which we need to attend. When it comes to our money dilemmas, looking inside is both the way in and the way out!

Be sure you include reflections in your journal on what happened when you took new actions in your money life. Ask yourself:

- How did taking your actions feel to you?
- Did your actions bring you further insights?
- Did they open up other possible steps you want to take?

APPENDIX
Resources for Action

Here's a list of resources to help you explore and educate yourself further about money matters. Be sure to search for other titles and websites that speak to your needs as online resources change frequently and sites specifically geared for women are bound to multiply.

Be aware that almost all websites are commercially supported and are marketing tools for a person, company, or profession. Investigate the Internet using the search terms: women, money, finance, or financial literacy to find helpful sites not included here.

I invite you to my website, www.emotionalcurrency.com where you will find an updated resource list along with other materials about women and money and a place for you to share what you've learned about your inner money life.

MONEY MANAGEMENT

Books

Smart Women Finish Rich: 9 Steps to Achieving Financial Security and Funding Your Dreams by David Bach

Girl, Get Your Money Straight: A Sister's Guide to Healing Your Bank Account and Funding Your Dreams in 7 Simple Steps by Glinda Bridgforth

The Money Therapist: A Woman's Guide to Creating a Healthy Financial Life by Marcia Brixey

Your Money or Your Life: Transforming Your Relationship with Money and Achieving Financial Independence by Joe Dominguez and Vicki Robin

Raising Financially Fit Kids by Joline Godfrey

The Wall Street Journal Guide to Understanding Personal Finance by Kenneth M. Morris

Women and Money: Owning the Power to Control Your Destiny by Suze Orman

Prince Charming Isn't Coming: How Women Get Smart About Money by Barbara Stanny

Secrets of Six-Figure Women: Surprising Strategies to Up Your Earnings and Change Your Life by Barbara Stanny

On My Own Two Feet: A Modern Girl's Guide to Personal Finance by Manisha Thakor and Sharon Kedar

Get Financially Naked: How to Talk Money with Your Honey by Manisha Thakor and Sharon Kedar

Websites

The learning center on the Women's Financial Network at Siebert website: www.wfn.com

Emotional Currency: www.emotionalcurrency.com

Your Money or Your Life: www.yourmoneyoryourlife.org

National Endowment for Financial Education: www.smartaboutmoney.com

Suze Orman: www.suzeorman.com

MSN Money: www.moneycentral.msn.com

The Wall Street Journal: www.online.wsj.com/home-page

Group

Debtors Anonymous

MONEY STORIES

Books

The Secret Currency of Love: The Unabashed Truth About Women, Money, and Relationships edited by Hilary Black

Nickled and Dimed: On (Not) Getting By in America by Barbara Ehrenreich

Money Changes Everything: Twenty-two Writers Tackle the Last Taboo with Tales of Sudden Windfalls, Staggering Debts, and Other Surprising Turns of Fortune edited by Jenny Offill and Elissa Schappell

Money, A Memoir: Women, Emotions, and Cash by Liz Perle

Without A Net: The Female Experience of Growing Up Working Class edited by Michelle Tea

MONEY AND SPIRIT

Books

It's Not About the Money: Unlock Your Money Type to Achieve Spiritual and Financial Abundance by Brent Kessel

Seven Stages of Money Maturity: Understanding the Spirit and Value of Money in Your Life by George Kinder

The Way of Woman: Awakening the Perennial Feminine by Helen Luke

Money and the Meaning of Life by Jacob Needleman

The Energy of Money: A Spiritual Guide to Financial and Personal Fulfillment by Maria Nemeth

The Soul of Money: Transforming Your Relationship with Money and Life by Lynne Twist

MONEY AND SOCIETY

Books

The Real Wealth of Nations: Creating A Caring Economics by Riane Eisler

The Gift: Imagination and the Erotic Life of Property by Lewis Hyde

The Story of Stuff: How Our Obsession with Stuff Is Trashing the Planet, Our Communities, and Our Health—and a Vision for Change by Annie Leonard

Cheap: The High Cost of Discount Culture by Ellen Ruppel Shell

Websites

Secret History of the Credit Card on the Frontline website: www.pbs.org/wgbh/pages/frontline/shows/credit/more/rise.html

The Story of Stuff video by Annie Leonard and website: www.storyofstuff.com

What Would Jesus Buy? DVD and Reverend Billy's website: www.revbilly.com

Robert Reich: www.robertreich.org

PHILANTHROPY

Books

Inspired Philanthropy: Creating Your Step-by-Step Guide to Creating a Giving Plan and Leaving a Legacy by Tracy Gary and Nancy Addess

Fundraising for Social Change by Kim Klein

Organizations and Websites

To compare your income with the rest of the world's population: Global Rich List: www.globalrichlist.com

Women's Funding Network website, with 165 worldwide women's foundations: www.womensfundingnetwork.org

Global Fund for Women: www.globalfundforwomen.org

Women for Women International: www.womenforwomen.org

Flow funding: www.flowfunding.org

To assess philanthropic organizations: www.charitynavigator.org and www2.guidestar.org

BIBLIOGRAPHY

Berry, Wendell. 2009. "Faustian Economics". In *The Best American Essays 2009*, edited by Mary Oliver. New York, New York: Mariner Books.

Brill, Betsy. 2009. "Women in Philanthropy". *Forbes.com*, August 18. www.forbes.com/2009/08/18/brill-women-philanthropy-intelligent-investing-wealth.html

Brizendine, MD, Louann. 2006. *The Female Brain*. New York, New York: Broadway Books.

Broucek, Francis J. 1991. *Shame and the Self*. New York, New York: Guilford Press.

Collins, Gail. 2009. *When Everything Changed: The Amazing Journey of American Women from 1960 to the Present*. New York, New York: Little, Brown and Company.

Cushman, Philip. 1995. *Constructing the Self, Constructing America: A Cultural History of Psychotherapy*. Reading, Massachusetts: Addison-Wesley.

Damasio, Antonio. 1994, 2005. *Descartes' Error: Emotion, Reason, and the Human Brain*. New York, New York: Penguin Books.

Dominguez, Joe and Vicki Robin. 1992. *Your Money or Your Life: Transforming Your Relationship with Money and Achieving Financial Independence*. New York, New York: Penguin Books.

Eisler, Riane. 1987. *The Chalice and the Blade: Our History, Our Future*. San Francisco: Harper and Row.

Eisler, Riane. 2007. *The Real Wealth of Nations: Creating A Caring Economics*. San Francisco, California: Berrett-Koehler Publishers.

Flinders, Carol Lee. 2002. *Rebalancing the World: Why Women Belong and Men Compete and How to Restore the Ancient Equilibrium*. New York, New York: Harper Collins.

Gilligan, Carol, and David A. J. Richards. 2009. *The Deepening Darkness: Patriarchy, Resistance, and Democracy's Future.* Cambridge, England: Cambridge University Press.

Heineman, Sue. 1996. *Timelines of American Women's History.* New York, New York: Perigee.

Hill, Gareth. 1992. *Masculine and Feminine: The Natural Flow of Opposites in the Psyche.* Boston, Massachusetts: Shambhala.

Hyde, Lewis. 1979. *The Gift: Imagination and the Erotic Life of Property.* New York, New York: Vintage.

Kessler-Harris, Alice. 2004. "Gender and the American experience." Lecture at the Chautauqua Institution. Chautauqua, New York, July 14.

Lui, Meizhu, Barbara Robles, Betsy Leondar-Wright, Rose Brewer, and Rebecca Adamson, with United for a Fair Economy. 2006. *The Color of Wealth: The Story Behind the U.S. Racial Wealth Divide.* New York, New York: The New Press.

Luke, Helen. 1995. *The Way of Woman: Awakening the Perennial Feminine.* New York, New York: Doubleday.

Martin, Sara. 2008. "Money is the Top Stressor for Americans." *Monitor on Psychology,* 30(1), 28-29.

Needleman, Jacob. 1994. *Money and the Meaning of Life.* New York, New York: Crown Books.

Ulanov, Ann. 1971. *The Feminine in Jungian Psychology and in Christian Theology.* Evanston, Illinois: Northwestern University Press.

Ulanov, Ann and Barry. 1998. *Cinderella and Her Sisters: The Envied and the Envying.* Einsiedein: Switzerland: Daimon Verlag.

Wertheimer, Barbara Mayer. 1977. *We Were There: The Story of Working Women in America.* New York, New York: Pantheon Books.

ABOUT THE AUTHOR

❦

A PSYCHOTHERAPIST AND COUPLES COUNSELOR for more than twenty-five years, Dr. Kate Levinson has led Emotional Currency™ workshops on women's emotional and psychological relationship to money since 2000 in California, Washington, and Minnesota. Dr. Levinson currently works with individuals and couples in her private practice in Oakland, California, and is on the supervising and teaching faculty at The Psychotherapy Institute. She frequently lectures, teaches, and writes on the psychological aspects of money. In addition, Dr. Levinson owns and operates an independent bookstore, with her husband, in Point Reyes Station, California. Visit emotionalcurrency.com for more information.

Photo by Aya Brackett

INDEX